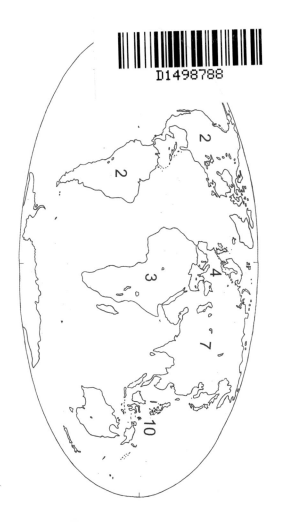

D1498788

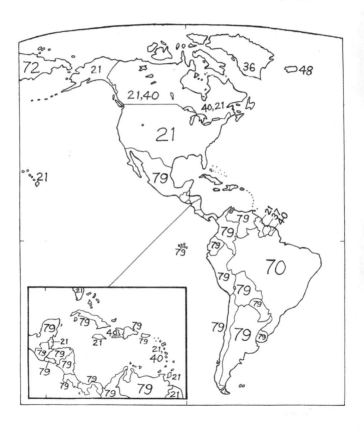

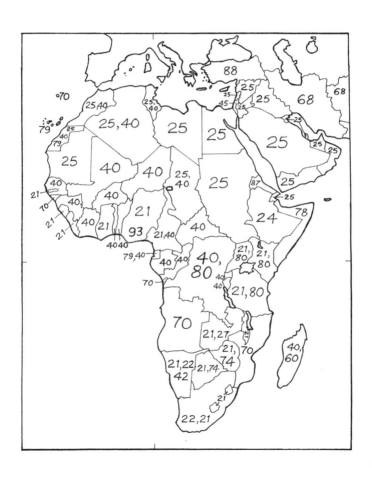

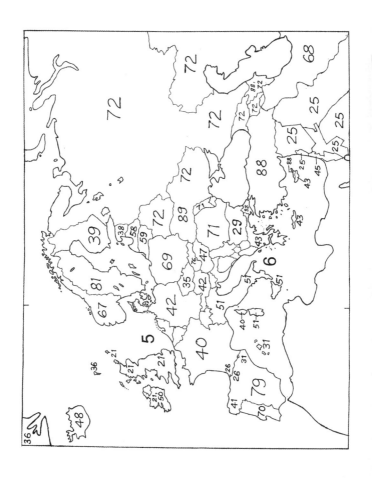

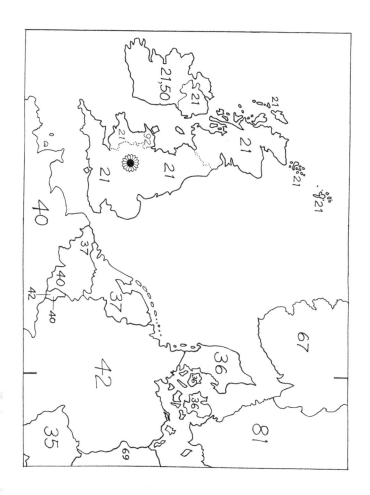

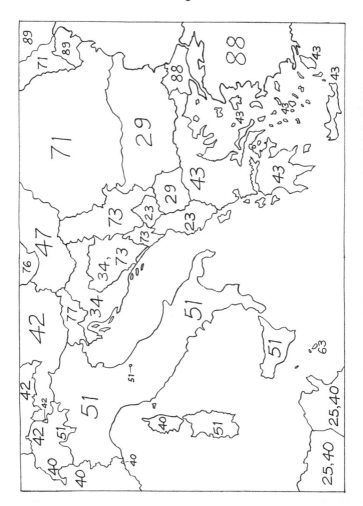

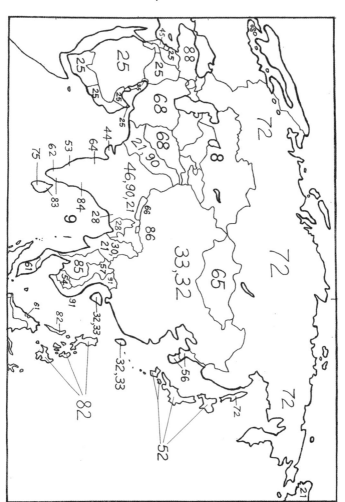

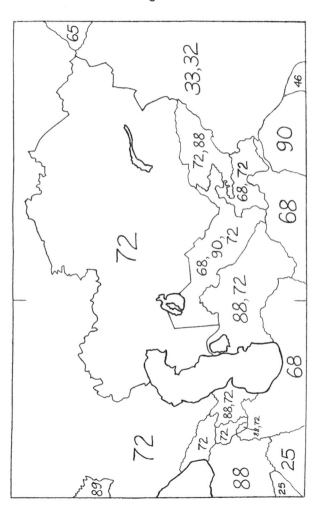

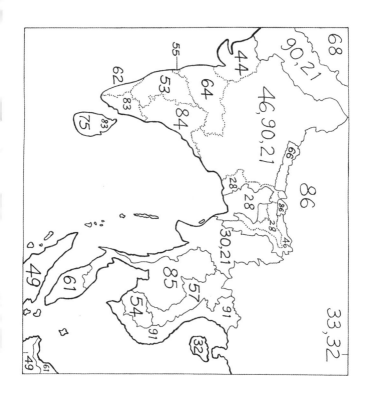

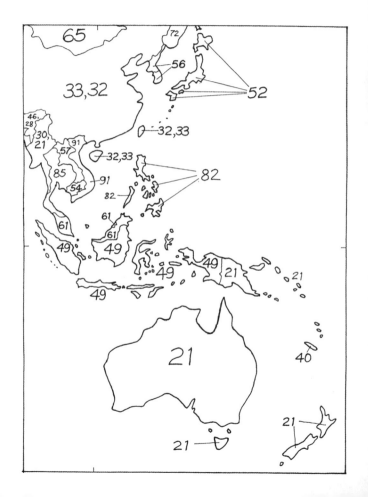

VEGAN PASSPORT

By George D Rodger

and over 100 other vegans & friends worldwide

First edition published July 1996

Second edition published June 2005

Third edition published February 2010

ISBN 978-0-907337-32-4

Printed on recycled paper by HSW Print

Cover design - www.doughnutdesign.co.uk

"If all else fails" illustrations by Diane Fisher

Published by The Vegan Society, Donald Watson House, 21 Hylton Street, Hockley, Birmingham B18 6HJ, United Kingdom (Tel 0121 523 1730)

All translations are believed to be accurate and are printed in good faith. The Vegan Society cannot accept liability for the consequences of any error in translation.

Pages 22, 29, 50, 57, 60, 65, 78 are used by permission of the Nederlandse Vegetariërsbond.

CONTENTS

HOW TO USE THIS BOOK

When visiting a restaurant, show your waiter/waitress the relevant page of this book, and ask him/her to read it. Do not attempt to pronounce the text yourself! If you are invited to a private home for a meal, show your host/hostess the relevant page well in advance. If booking a hotel by post or email, send a copy of the relevant page. Please note that several languages may be used in the place you are visiting, so you may be able to offer the reader a choice of languages. See the maps or the index.

怎么使用这本书

上餐馆时，让侍应生详细阅读书中相关的页面。别尝试自己读出文本。如果你被邀请到私人家中用餐，事先让邀请您的主人或女主人详细阅读书中相关的页面。如果你以邮件或电子邮件预定旅馆，务必拷贝一份书中相关的页面给旅馆。请注意您所访问的地方可能会使用多种语言。因此您或许可以提供多种语言让对方选择。请参考书中相关的地图或索引。

CÓMO USAR ESTE LIBRO

Cuando vaya a comer a un restaurante enseñe al camarero/a la camarera la página pertinente de este libro y pidale que la lea. ¡No trate de pronunciar el texto usted mismo! Si le invitan a comer en una casa particular asegúrese que sus anfitriones hayan leido con antelación la página adecuada. Si hace una reserva de hotel por correo envieles una copia del texto. Tenga en cuenta que pueden hablar varias lenguas en el lugar que usted visite y debe dejar al lector elegir el idioma más adecuada. Ver los mapas y el índice.

كيفية استعمال هذا الكتاب

عندما تقوم بزيارة أحد المطاعم، دل خادم أو خادمة المائدة على الصفحة المناسبة في هذا الكتاب واطلب منه أو منها قراءة الصفحة. لا تحاول قراءة النص بنفسك! إذا تمت دعوتك لتناول الطعام في منزل خاص، دل مضيفك أو مضيفتك على الصفحة المناسبة مقدما. إذا كنت تحجز في أحد الفنادق عبر البريد أو البريد الإلكتروني، ارسل نسخة عن الصفحة المناسبة. الرجاء الملاحظة أنه قد تستخدم لغات متعددة في المكان الذي تزوره وأنه قد يكون بإمكانك توفير خيار لغات أخرى للقارئ. انظر إلى الخرائط أو الفهرس.

COMMENT UTILISER CE PASSEPORT

Au restaurant, montrez la page adéquate à votre serveur/serveuse, et demandez-lui de la lire. N'essayez pas de prononcer vous-même le texte! Si vous êtes invité(e) à déjeuner ou à dîner chez les particuliers, montrez bien à l'avance la page adéquate à votre hôte. Si vous réservez un hôtel par correspondance ou par 'e-mail', envoyez une copie de la page adequate. Notez que plusieurs langues peuvent être utilisées sur le lieu de votre visite, aussi vous pouvez laisser le choix à votre interlocuteur en lui proposant les différentes langues. Voir les cartes et l'index.

この本の使い方

海外のレストランに行った際は、この本の該当するページを給仕人に呈示して下さい。あなた自身が声を出して読もうとしなくていいのです！だれかの家のお食事に招かれた際は、そのご主人に前もって該当するページを読んでもらって下さい。郵便や電子メールでホテルを予約する際は、該当するページのコピーを送ってください。訪問地によっては、数カ国語が使われているかもしれません。この本はそれに対応できます。地図と索引がありますので、読者に該当するページを読んでもらって下さい

COMO USAR ESTE LIVRO

Quando for a um restaurante, mostre ao empregado/à empregada de mesa a página apropriada deste livro e peça-lhes que a leiam. Não tente ser você a pronunciar as palavras do texto! Se o/a convidarem para uma refeição numa casa particular, mostre a página apropriada à pessoa que o/a vai receber, com bastante antecedência. Se fizer uma reserva de hotel por correio normal ou por correio electrónico, envie uma cópia da página apropriada. Por favor note que podem usar-se várias línguas no lugar que está a visitar, podendo assim oferecer ao leitor uma escolha de línguas. Consulte os mapas ou o índice.

जब आप भोजनालय कि मुलाकात ले, वेड्टर या वेड्ट्रेस को इस पत्रीका का उचित प्रुष्ठ दीखाऐ और उन्हे पढने के लीऐ अनुरोध करै. शब्दो का उच्चारण करने का प्रयास ना करे! अगर आपको कीसी के नीजी आवास पे भोजन के लीए आमन्त्रित कीया गया है तो आपके मेजबान को उचित प्रुष्ठ अग्रिमता से बतादें. यदि आप होटेल का बुकिंग डाक या ई-मेईल से कर रहे है तो उचित प्रुष्ठ की कापी भेजें. क्रिप्या ये ध्यान रखें की आप जो स्थान की मुलाकात ले रहे है, हो सकता है की वहां अनेक भाशांओ का प्रयोग हो रहा हो, इस स्थिति मे आप वाचक को अनेक भाशांओ का प्रस्ताव रख सकते है. क्रिप्या नक्शा या सुचकांक देखें.

КАК ВОСПОЛЬЗОВАТЬСЯ ЭТОЙ КНИГОЙ

При посещении ресторана покажите официанту / официантке соответствующую страницу в книге и попросите прочитать текст. Не пытайтесь сами произнести этот текст! Если вас пригласили в гости на угощение, заранее покажите хозяину или хозяйке соответствующую страницу. При бронировании гостиницы по обычной или электронной почте, пошлите копию соответствующей страницы. Пожалуйста, заметьте, что в месте вашего посещения могут использоваться несколько языков, поэтому вы можете предложить человеку, который будет читать текст, на выбор несколько языков, на которых написан текст. Смотрите карты указателя.

HINWEISE ZUR BENUTZUNG DIESES BUCHS

Beim Restaurantbesuch bitten Sie den Kellner bzw. die Kellnerin, die entsprechende Seite dieses Buches zu lesen (der Aussprache wegen ist dies meist besser als der Versuch, den Text vorzulesen). Bei privaten Einladungen oder einer Hotelbuchung können Sie auch schon im Voraus eine Kopie der jeweiligen Seite überreichen bzw. verschicken. In mehrsprachigen Ländern bietet es sich an, die Seiten mehrerer Sprachen zu verwenden (siehe Karten oder Index).

এই বইখানার ব্যবহারের নির্দেশ

কোন রেষ্টুরেন্টে গেলে ওয়েটার বা ওয়েটরেসদের এই বইখানার প্রাসঙ্গিক পৃষ্ঠাটা দেখাবেন এবং ওদের নিজেদের পড়ে নিতে বলবেন । উদ্যোগি হয়ে কখনো নিজে পড়তে যাবেন না । কোন বাড়ীতে যদি নিমন্ত্রিত হয়ে যান তাহলে বাড়ীর লোকদের বেশ খানিকটা আগেই প্রাসঙ্গিক পৃষ্ঠা খানা দেখাবেন । যদি ই-মেইল বা পৌষ্টে হোটেল বুক করেন তাহলে বুকিং এর সময় সেই প্রয়োজনীয় পৃষ্ঠাখানা পাঠানো উচিত হবে । মনে রাখবেন যেসব জায়গাতে যাবেন সেখানে হয়ত বিভিন্ন ভাষায় বক্তব্য প্রকাশের সুযোগ থাকবে । মেপ অথবা সূচীপত্রের দিকে নজর রাখবেন ।

KIEL UZI ĈI TION LIBRON

Kiam vi vizitas restoracion, montru al via kelnero/ino la ĝustan paĝon en ĉi tiu libron, kaj petu lin/ŝin legi ĝin. Neniam provu vi mem prononci la teksto! Se vi estos invitata manĝi ĉe privata hejmo, montru la ĝustan paĝon al via gastiganto en bona tempo. Kiam vi rezervas hotelon per poŝto aŭ 'e-mail', sendu kopion de la ĝusta paĝo. Rimarku ke eble pluraj lingvoj estos uzataj kie vi vizitos, do vi eble povos proponi al leganto elekton de paĝo. Vidu mapojn aŭ indekson.

18

ACKNOWLEDGEMENTS

George Rodger and The Vegan Society wish to thank the following contributors, who made this book possible. (Also anyone who has been inadvertently omitted!)

Agné Jankauskaite, Alex Bourke, Alka Parikh, Amir Kashiv, Ariadne Fern, Armando Bertolino, Arthur Chang, Asif Parvez, Avi Yaacov, Barbara Staples, Básel Péter, Betsan Evans, Betül Işık, Brian Burnett, Carmen Areses, Charley Roberts, Chris Dixon, Chuthikan Guwan Elder, Coby Siegenthaler, Corina Hll Poh Chuo, David Chan, Doreen Bliss, Duncan Toms, Edna Eliot-McColl, Ewa K Suskiewicz, Francisco Martin, Fred Opot, Gabriel Partos, Galina Appleby, Ganesh Shankar Muthukrishnan, Gianbattista Montagna, Gity Salehzadeh, Harry Mather, Heather Green, Heidrun Leisenheimer, Henk de Jong, Hiroko Tsuchiya, Ingeberg Elvers, Jasmina Bašaneže, Javad Mirhashemi, Jennifer Lester, Jevgenija Sundejeva, Joaquim Palau i Selva, Jogabrata Raha, Johanna Best, John Darmanin, Juanita Eskubi, Julia Hope Jacquel, Khunarat Lai, Kirsten Jungsberg, Lázár Helen, Leah C Lau, Lilia Fabretto, Loore Emilie Raav, Mania Kingdom, Marek Voršilka, Margarita Viiderfeld, Maria Teresa Andoñgo, Martin Janek, Martti Bergestad, Matthias Schojohann, Mauricio Passer, Michal Podogrodski, Moira Chan, Monda Konayuma, Naama Harel, Nabanita Mitra, Nanji Eastham, Neil Raha, Nigel Winter, Nova Doba, Pål Thorbjørnsen, Patricia Pérez, Patricia Tricker, Pekala Károly, Pekala Noor, Peter Chadamwoyo, Prithwis Banerjee, Purminder Singh Gill, Rafic Kreidi, Ranjit Konkar, Raz Ofer, Rochelle Del Gunter, Ronak Pandya, Rosamund Raha, Ruhama Itzhaky, Samuel Olugbenga King, Samar Al-Afandi, Santoshni Perera, Sarah Lane, Shankar Narayan, Sían Meredudd, Sözen İsmail, Stéphane Hennion, Steve Kingdom, Steve O'Hagan, Stewart Elder, Suzanne Trauffer, Tamura Miyuki, Tanya Perez, Tay Cheng-Hui (Max), Ted Kim Yun-Kuk, Teresa Dangerfield, Theresa Bommelin, Thomas Čuk, Timoleos Butshi, Tony D'Souza, Tracy Macheta, Tsai Hsing Hung, Ulla Troëng, Vanessa Clarke, Vera Muzikova, Verity Hunt-Sheppard, Vijay Kumar Raghaviah, Vincent Berraud, Willy Lee, Yang Jun Yu, Yasuyo Ito, Zoran Cica.

Also five anonymous contributors.

Thanks to Louise Wallis, who had the original idea!

Thanks to the Nederlandse Vegetariërsbond for permission to use their copyright material.

Maps, aircraft drawing and page decorations by Jorge Hrothgar.

Welsh Dragon by David Chan.

Esperanto Globe by Lilia Fabretto, TEVA.

Further offers of languages, and corrections or improvements to existing language pages are always welcome. See page 95.

LIST OF LANGUAGES

PLEASE READ THIS

I am a vegan / We are vegans

On principle, vegans do not eat anything of animal origin, - for the benefit of people, animals and the environment.

So we do not eat: meat (including minced meat, sausages, etc.), poultry (including chicken), fish, shellfish, or other animal products such as honey, eggs, milk, butter, cheese, or other dairy produce.

But we do eat: potatoes, rice, pasta (non-egg), beans, vegetables, tomatoes, fruits, nuts, mushrooms; breads or pastries made without animal fat; cereals and cereal products, etc.

Soups and sauces may be made with vegetable stock but not with meat or chicken extracts. Only pure vegetable oil or pure vegetable margarine may be used in cooking, not butter or any other animal fat.

Please, can you provide a meal which meets our requirements?

THANK YOU VERY MUCH

Ek is 'n veganiet.

Dit beteken dat ek uit oortuiging niks van dierlike oorsprong eet nie.

Ek et dus geen: vleis (insluitende maalvleis, alle soorte wors, ens.), vis, garnale, mossels, pluimvee (insluitende hoender), of ander dierlike produkte soos melk, kaas, eiers of ander suimelprodukte.

Eke et wel: groente, aartappels, tamaties, neute, rys, vrugte, graan en graanprodukte, ens.

Sop en sous mag met groente-aftreksel gemaak word, maar nie met vleis- of visekstrak nie.

Daar mag alleen met plantardige olie of margarine gebak of gebraai word en nie met botter of ander dierlike vette nie.

Baie Dankie

JU LUTEMI LEXONI SA MË POSHTË

Unë jam barngrënës - Ne jemi barngrënës (Vigan).

Parimi i njerëzve të grupit «Vigan» (barngrënësve fanatik) është të mos hanë fare prodhime me origjinë shtazore në dobi të kafshëve, të njerëzve dhe të ambjentit.

Nuk hamë: mishin (dhe gjellët e gatuara prej mishi si qofte, suflaqa, sallam etj) pula dhe të tjera të këtij lloji, peshk dhe prodhime të tjera deti (si ohtapodhi, kallamarët, ngjalat etJ). Gjithashta nuk hamë të gjitha prodhimet shtazore dhe nënproduktet e tyre si mjalti, vezët, qumështi, gjalpi, djathi dhe nënproduktet e tjera te qumështit. Përsërisim që nuk hamë asnjë gjellë e cila përmban produkte ushqimore me origjinë shtazore.

Ne hamë: patate, oriz, makarona (që nuk përmbajnë brënda vezë), fasule, lakërishte, domate, fruta, arra, kërpudha, bukë, dhe brumëra që përmbajnë yndyrna me prejardhje shtazore. Hamë supra të përgatitura pa produkte shtazore, me thjerrëza, me fasule si dhe sallatra pa djathë, majonezë etj.

Supa dhe sallata nuk duhet të përmbajnë produkte mishi ose yndyrna shtazore. Vetëm vaji vegjetal ose margarina bimore e pastër mund të perdoret për gatim, par jo gjalpi ose yndyrnat e tjera shtazore.

Ju lutemi të na servirni asortimente që përputhen me kërkesat tona.

JU FALEMINDERIT

አገልግሎን. ምሁን እንስለ

ኤኔ | ኤኖ ለጋ የእንስሳ ውጤቶች እኢዎፎ ወፈርም የእሳዘሮት
እንክፍለው

በመሐለኛ ከለወጋ ለእንስሶችና ለወጋንዎርነት እናገሮ ያቆም
ሲገባ የእንስሳ ክጋ ወፈርም ከእንስሳ የሚገኙ የምግብ
ምንጮች እንበሉም።

ገዘ ለታች የሚከተሉትን እንበሉም
የተለያዩ የለጋ እዐንዋቶን፣ የእንቁላል ዝርያዎች
ፍሬ፣ ፍሬዎ ለለጆ ወንጀሙ የእሳ ዘሮት ወፈርም ከለ
የእንስሳ ወ ጤቶችን ለምለሌ ሮጌ፣ እንቁላል፣ ቅቤ
እርሳ ወፈርም ከወተት የሚገኙ የምግብ ወፈርም የሰጠንን ጎሮቶን
እንወገላለን።

ቀምንለፈሁ ጎጎሮች ከዘ ለታች የሚከተሉትን

ዱኖች ፋዝ፡ ፓሰታ (ከእንቁላል ወፈርም እንቁላል የለለሁ)
ባቄላ እትክልቶች ተወጥታ ፍራፍሬ እቅላ እንጉሎ
ረከበ ወፈርም ንፍ የእንስሳ ስብ ወፈርም እንቁላል የለለው
ቅርባ ወጋ ከእንቁላት የተሰራ በጋ ዓከወሆ ዓለ
የሌለው።! የእንቁላት ዘይት ወፈርም የእንቁላት
ማርጋሪን ቅቤ ከመሰለአኛ ወበጠታም ሰጋጃል
ቅባ ወፈርም ስጋ የእንስሳ ቅባት የሌለው.

ከአገልግሎ ከኬል የተጠቀሱትን ወፈርዝምረት የሚያዮለ
የምግብ ዝርዝር ከሚዘጋጅት ከቅርብል።

ከምስጋና ጋር

الرجاء قراءة التالي

أنا نباتي قح/ أنا نباتية قح ـ نحن نباتيون قح

المبدأ الأساسي للنباتيون أنهم لايأكلون أي شيء مصدره حيواني، من أجل مصلحة الإنسان والحيوان والبيئة.

لذلك لانأكل: اللحم الأحمر (بما في ذلك اللحم المفروم ، والنقانق، إلخ.)، لحوم الدواجن (بما في ذلك الدجاج)، السمك، المحار، أو أي منتج حيواني مثل العسل، البيض، الزبدة، الجبن، والحليب ومشتقاته.

لكن نحن نأكل: البطاطا، والأرز، والمعكرونة (الخالية من البيض)، البقول بأنواعها، الخضار، البندورة، الفواكه، المكسرات، الفطر، الخبز والمعجنات الخالية من أي دهن حيواني، الحبوب ومشتقاتها، إلخ.

الشوربات والصلصات المحضرة باستخدام خلاصة الخضار فقط وليس خلاصة اللحم أو الدجاج.
فقط يمكن استخدام الزيوت النباتية والزيوت النباتية المهدرجة في الطبخ، وليس الزبد أو الدهن الحيواني.

الرجاء تقديم وجبة طعام ملائمة لطلباتنا؟
شكراً جزيلاً

MESEDEZ, HURRENGOA IRAKURRI

Landare-jale sutsua naiz / Landare-jale sutsuak gara

Hasteko, landare-jale sutsuak garenok ez dugu abere jatorria duten elikagairik jaten, pertsonen, animalien eta inguru giroaren mesedarako.

Beraz, guk ez dugu honakoa jaten: haragia (haragi gihartsua, saltxitxak, e.a. barne), oilotegietako animaliak (oilaskoa barne), arraina, krustazeo edo beste abere produktuak eztia, arraultza, esnea, gurina, gazta eta esnekiak bezala.

Baina honakoa jan dezakegu: patatak, arroza, pasta (arraultza barik), indabak, barazkiak, tomateak, frutak, fruitu lehorrak, perretxikoak; ogie edo pastelak animali koiperik gabe; zaerealak e.a.

Zopa eta saltsa barazki osagaiekin eginda baina ez haragi edota oilasko erauzkinarekin. Sukaldaritzan landare-olio purua edo landare-margarina purua bakarrik erabiliko da, ez gurin ezta beste animlu koiperik ere.

Posible izango litzateke baldintza hauek dituzten jangalak ematea?

MILA ESKER

Mukwai belengeni:

Ndimu vegan / tulima vegans.

Ama vegan tabalya ifilifyonse ififuma ku nama, pakuti bafwe abantu, ifinama ne chalo.

So tatulya:

inama (ukubikako na mince, na sosegi), ifyoni (ukubikako ne inkoko), isabi, nangu ifili fyonse ifipangwa nefinama ifyapala ubuchi, amani, umukaka, bata, cheesi, nangu ifililfyonse ifipangwa no mukaka.

Koma tulalya:

amapoteto, rice, pasta (yabula amani), chilemba, umusalu, tomato, ifisabo, inseke, ubowa, breadi nangu ifyafulawa ukwabula ukupangila amafuta yafinama, cereals (ifyapala amataba) ne ifyapangwa nama cereals (ifyapala ubwali, polege).

Supu na sosi yapangwa na stock ya musalu noti inami nangu inkoko. Oilo nagula amafuta yapangwa no musalu kuti yabomfiwa ukwipika, noti bata nangu amafuta ya nama.

Mukwai pekanyeni ifykulya ngefyo filefwaikwa.

Twatasha.

দয়া করে এইটা পড়ুন

আমি vegan (ভিগান) / আমরা vegans (ভিগানস)

অর্থাৎ আমরা জন্তুদের থেকে প্রাপ্ত কোন উপাদেয় খাদ্য খাই না ।
আমরা বিশ্বাস করি যে এতেই মানবজাতি, জন্তুদের ও পরিবেশের মঙ্গল ।

আমরা নিম্নলিখিত খাদ্যগুলি খেতে পারি না :

- মাংস মাছ ডিম মধু দুধ এবং দুধের থেকে তৈরি খাদ্য (যেমন মিষ্টি দই, ঘরেপাতা দই, ঘোল, রাবড়ি)
- ঘি এবং ঘি থেকে তৈরি খাদ্য (যেমন ঘিতে ভাঁজা মিষ্টি)
- মাখন বা মাখন যেসব খাবারে ব্যবহার করা হয় (যেমন স্যান্ডউইচ)
- ছানা এবং ছানার থেকে তৈরি খাদ্য (যেমন মিষ্টি, ছানার ডালনা)
- আইসক্রীম, কুলফি, মিল্কশেক কেক, বিস্কিট (যেঁটায় মাখন ব্যবহার করা হয়েছে), মিল্ক-ব্রেড

- দুধ দেওয়া চা বা কফি তাহলে আমরা কি খাই?

- সবরকম তরকারি, ফল, জল সর্বত, ডাবের জল
- দুধ বিনা চা বা কফি ভেজিটেবল অয়েল এ ভাঁজা মিষ্টি যেঁটা দুধ থেকে তৈরি না (যেমন লাড্ডু)

যেকোন উপাদেয় খাদ্য ভাঁজতে আপনারা ঘি বা মাখন ব্যবহার করবেন না ।
ভেজিটেবল অয়েলএ ভাঁজা খাদ্য আমরা শুধু গ্রহন করি ।
কোন মিষ্টিতে আপনারা রাংতা দেবেন না ।
দয়া করে আমাদের এমন একটি আহার দেবেন যাতে আমাদের বিশ্বাস অটুট থাকে ।

ধন্যবাদ

Аэ съм веганиет / веганиетка

По убеждение не ям нищо от животински произход.

Не ям: месо, риба, раци, миди, птици (пиле), животински продукти: кълцано месо, салсм, наденици и др., а също и мляко, сирене, яйца и други млечни продукти.

Мога да ям: зеленчуци, картофи, домати, орехи, гъби, ориз, плодове, зърнени и зърнени продукти.

Супи, сосове, бульони и др. не трябва да са приготвени от месо, пиле и т.н., а само от зеленчуци. Пържени или печени ястия притотвени само с растително олио или маргарин, но не с краве масло или животински масти.

ကျေးဇူးပြု၍ ဤစာကိုဖတ်ပေးပါ။

ကျွန်တော်၊ ကျွန်မတို့သည် ငါး၊ ကြက်ဥ၊ နွားနို့ကဲ့သို့သော အသားများပင် မစား သော သက် သတ်လွတ်သမားများဖြစ်ပါသည်။

အခြေခံအားဖြင့် လူသား၊ တိရိစ္ဆာန်နှင့် ပတ်ဝန်းကျင်ကို အကျိုးပြုရန်အလို့ငှာ တိရိစ္ဆာန်မှ ထုတ် လုပ်သော မည်သည့်အစားအစာများကိုမှ မစားသော သက်သတ်လွတ် သမားများဖြစ်ပါသည်။

ထို့ကြောင့် အောက်ပါအရာများကို ကျွန်ုပ်တို့ မစားသုံးပါ။

အသား (နုပ်နင်စည်းထားသောအသား၊ အသားအချောင်း အစရှိသောအသားများ)၊ ကြက်သား၊ ဘဲသား၊ ငန်းသား၊ ကြက်ဆင်သား စသော အသားများ၊ ငါး၊ ပင်လယ်စာများ၊ တိရိစ္ဆာန် မှထုတ်လုပ်သော ဗျာရည်၊ ကြက်ဥ၊ နွားနို့၊ ထောပတ်၊ ချိစ် နှင့် အခြားသော တိရိစ္ဆာန်မှ ထုတ်လုပ်သော နို့ထွက် ပစ္စည်း များ တို့ဖြစ်ပါ သည်။

သို့သော် ကျွန်ုပ်တို့ အောက်ပါအရာများကိုစားသုံးပါသည်။

အာလူး၊ ထမင်း၊ ကြက်ဥမပါသော ပါစတာ (အီတာလီခေါက်ဆွဲတစ်မျိုး)၊ ပဲများ၊ အသီးအရွက်များ၊ ခရမ်းချဉ်သီး၊ အသီးများ၊ သစ်သီးစေ့များ၊ မှို၊ တိရိစ္ဆာန် အဆီ မပါသော ပေါင်မုန့် နှင့် အချိုမုန့် များ စီရိရယ်ကဲ့သို့သော အစားအစာ များ တို့ ပင်ဖြစ်ပါသည်။

ဟင်းရည်နှင့် ဆော့စ်များ မှာ ဟင်းရွက်အဆီအနှစ်နှင့် ပြုလုပ်ပြီး ကြက်သား၊ အသား များ နှင့်ပြု လုပ်ထားခြင်းမဟုတ်ရပါ။ ဟင်းချက်ရာတွင်လည်း ဟင်းသီး ဟင်းရွက်ဆီ၊ ဟင်းသီး ဟင်းရွက် မာဂျရင်းသော အသုံးပြုရမည်ဖြစ်ပြီး၊ ထောပတ် (သို့မဟုတ်) အ ခြားသော တိရိစ္ဆာန်ဆီများကို အသုံးမပြုရပါ။

ကျေးဇူးပြု၍ ကျွန်ုပ်တို့၏ဝါလိုအပ်ချက်နှင့် ကိုက်ညီသော အစားအစာများကိုပေးပါ။

ကျေးဇူးတင်ပါသည်။

SIUSPLAU LLEGEIXI AIXO:

Soc vegà / Som vegans

En principi, els vegans no consumeixen res que provingui d'un animal, pel benefici de les persones, els animals i el medi ambient.

Així que no mengem pas: Ni carn (incloent carn picada, salsitxes, botifarres, cansalada, etc..), ni aviram (incloent el pollastre), ni peix, ni marisc ni altres productes d'origen animal com la mel, ous, llet, mantega, formatge i els seus derivats.

Però mengem: Patates, arròs, pasta (sense ou), llegums, hortalisses, tomàquets, fruita, fruits secs, bolets, tot tipus de pa (sense llet o mel), cereals, etc...

Podem usar i consumir caldos i salses fetes amb caldo vegetal, no d'origen animal.

Només podem emprar olis d'origen vegetal en la cocció d'aliments, en cap cas mantega o altres greixos d'origen animal.

Podrien doncs fer-nos un àpat que compleixi els nostres requisits dietètics siusplau?

MERCES

请详细阅读

我 / 我们是纯素食者

根据纯素食原则，为了人类、动物及自然环境的利益，纯素食者不食用任何含有动物成分的食物。

因此我们不食用：
肉类（包括肉酱、腊肠等），家禽（包括鸡、鸭、鹅、其他鸟类、牛、羊、猪等），野味（包括蛙、蛇等），海鲜（包括鱼、虾、蟹、贝、蚝、水母等），及任何含有动物成分的食物比如蜂蜜、蛋、乳、奶油、乳酪或其他乳酪制成品。

但我们食用：
薯类（如马铃薯、木薯、甘薯、番薯等），谷类（如米、麦、玉米等）及其制成品，面条（不含蛋），豆类，蔬菜，番茄，水果，坚果，菇类及不含动物脂肪的面包或糕点。

汤、羹及浆料可以用蔬菜或植物制成。但是不可使用肉类或鸡精等。烹饪时，只可使用纯植物油或纯植物人造黄油，不可使用奶油或其他动物脂肪。

请问您可以符合我们以上的要求为我们准备一餐吗？

非常感谢您

請 細 讀

我／我們是純素食主義者

原則上，純素食主義者不食用任何動物成份的食物－－以利益全人類、動物及天然的環境。

因此，我們不食用：

肉類（包括肉醬、臘腸等），家禽（包括雞、鴨、鵝、其他鳥類、豬、牛、羊等），蛙類、魚類、蚌類、蝦類、蠔、水母等及任何含有動物成份的產品如蜂蜜、蛋類、乳類、奶油、乳酪或其產品。

但是，我們有食用：

薯類（如馬鈴薯、木薯、甘薯、蕃薯等），穀類（如米、麥、玉蜀黍等），糕點（不含蛋），豆類、蔬菜、蕃茄、水果、堅果類、菇類、麵包餡餅（不含動物油或脂肪）等。
蔬菜或植物製成的湯、羹、醬或汁，但不可含有任何肉類成品或雞精等。烹飪時，只可使用純植物油或植物制奶油，不可使用動物油、脂肪或奶油。

請遵照以上的需求為我們準備一餐。   謝謝

MOLIMO PROČITAJTE OVU OBAVJEST

Ja sam vegan / mi smo vegani
(Strogi vegetarijanci)

Iz principa, vegani ne jedu namirnice životinjskog porijekla za bolju budućnost ljudi, životinja i prirode.

Mi ne jedemo: Meso (uključujući mljeveno meso, kobasice itd) perad (uključujući kokoš), ribu, školjke, druge životinjske proizvode na primjer med, jaja, jogurt, mlijeko, maslo, sir i druge mliječne proizvode.

Mi jedemo: Krumpir, rižu, tjesteninu (bez jaja), grašak, povrče, voče, bajame, orahe, gljive; kruh I slično ali bez životinjske masnoče, žitarice i žitarske proizvode; juhe i sosevi sa povrčem bez mesa i piletine.

Samo čisto vegetarijansko ulje ili vegetarijanski margarin može da se upotrebi u kuhanju, bez masla i ostalih životinjskih masnoča.

Molimo vas da pripremite jelo po ovim uputama.

HVALA

PROSÍM PŘEČTĚTE SI

Jsem vegán. / Jsem vegánka. / Jsme vegáni.

Principiálně vegáni nekonzumují nic, co je živočišného původu - ve prospěch lidí, zvířat a životního prostředi.

Nekonzumujeme tudíž: maso (ani ve formě sekané, párků či podobně), drůbež (kuřata nevyjímajíc), ryby, mořské živočichy a výrobky živočišneho původu jako jsou med, vejce, mléko, máslo, sýr a jiné mléčné výrobky.

Ale konzumujeme: brambory, těstoviny (bezvaječné), rýži, luštěniny, zeleninu, ovoce, ořechy, houby, chléb a pečivo vyrobené bez živočisného tuku, obilniny (jako ovesné vločky a jim podobne výrobky) atd.

Polévky a omáčky mohou být vyrobeny z potravin rostlinného původu, ale bez výtažků masa a drůbeže jako i vývaru. Jen čistý rostlinný olej nebo čistý rostlinný margarín může být použit při vaření, žádne máslo nebo jiný živočišný tuk.

Prosím nabídněte nám jídlo, které splňuje naše požadavky.

DĚKUJEME

VÆR VENLIG AT LÆSE DETTE:

Jeg er veganer / vi er veganere

Af princip, spiser veganere intet af animalsk oprindelse – til gavn for mennesker, dyr, og miljø.

Derfor spiser vi ikke: kød (incl. kødfars, pølser, osv.), fjerkræ (incl. kylling), fisk, skaldyr eller andre animalske produkter såsom honning, æg, mælk, smør, ost, eller andre mejeriprodukter.

Imidlertid spiser vi: kartofler, ris, pasta (uden æg), alle slags linser og bønner, grøntsager, tomater, frugt, nødder, champignon; brød og bagværk (lavet uden animalsk fedt, mælk og æg); korn og kornprodukter osv.

Supper og sovser kan laves med vegetabilsk bouillon – men ikke med kød- eller hønse- bouillon. Kun ren vegetabilsk olie eller ren plantemargarine, må bruges ved madlavningen ikke smør eller andet animalisk fedtstof.

Vær venlig at imødekomme disse beskedne krav under tilberedningen af min/vor mad.

MANGE TAK FOR HJÆLPEN

WILT U DIT AUB LEZEN

Ik ben veganist / Wij zijn veganisten

Uit principe eten veganisten geen voedsel van dierlijke oorsprong – ten voordele van mens, dier en milieu.

Dus eten wij het volgende niet: vlees (inclusief gehakt, worst, enz.), gevogelte (inclusief kip), vis, schelpdieren of andere dierlijke produkten zoals honing, eieren, melk, boter, kaas, yoghurt en andere zuivelprodukten.

Maar het volgende eten wij wel: aardappelen, rijst, pasta (zonder eieren), peulvruchten, groenten, tomaten, fruit, noten, champignons; brood en gebak zonder dierlijke vetten en produkten; granen en graanprodukten, enz.

Soepen en sauzen mogen van plantaardige bouillon (geen wei of melksuiker/lactose) worden gemaakt maar niet van vees-kip- of visbouillon. Alleen plantaardige oliën en vetten kunnen worden gebruikt voor koken, dus geen boter, ghee of andere dierlijke vetten.

Wilt u zo vriendlijk zijn om ons van een maaltijd te voorzien die aan onze voorwaarden voldoet.

HARTELIJK BEDANKT

Ma olen vegaanlane/ me oleme vegaanlased

(me sööme ainult taimseidtoite).

Vegaanlased on inimesed, kes ei söö loomset toitu ja seda vastutusest inimese, looma ja keskkonna ees.

Niisiis ei söö me : liha(ka mitte hakkliha, vorsti, sinki jne.), linnuliha (kana, part jne.), kala (ka mitte krabisid, teokarpe jne.), ka mitte toiduaineid, mis on loomset päritolu, näiteks piimatooteid (või, juust, kohupiim, jogurt jne.), loomseid rasvu (näiteks searasv), mune ja mett.

Aga me some: meeleldi kartuleid, riisi, nuudleid (ilma munata), kaunvilju (herned, oad, läätsed jne.), igat sorti puuvilju ja köögivilju, pähkleid ja seeni, samuti teraviljaooteid nagu näiteks leib ja muud küpsetised (ilma loomsete rasvaineteta) ja sojatooteid, näiteks tofu.

Kasutage suppide ja kastmete jaoks palun köögivilja-(aedvilja-) puljongit, (mitte liha- või kanapuljongit). Praadimiseks, keetmiseks ja küpsetamiseks kasutage palun puhtal kujul taimseid rasvu, mitte võid või muid loomseid rasvu. Margariini ilma piimsete lisanditeta jne.

Meil on hea meel, kui Te suutsite oma toidukorra ajal järgida meiepoolseid soovitusi!

SUUR TÄNU!

VOISITTEKO LUKEA SEURAAVAN

Olen vegaani / olemme vegaaneja

Vegaanit eivät periaatteesta syö eläinkunnasta peräisin olevia tuotteita. Mielestämme tämä koituu niin ihmisten, eläinten kuin ympäristönkin parhaaksi.

Emme siis syö lihaa (mukaanlukien jauhelihaa, makkaraa tms.), lintuja (mukaanlukien kanaa), kalaa, simpukoita, rapuja tai muita eläinperäisiä tuotteita kuten hunajaa, munaa, maitoa, voita, juustoa tai muita maitotuotteita.

Sen sijaan syömme perunoita, riisiä, pastaa (jossa ei ole munaa), papuja, vihanneksia, tomaatteja, hedelmiä, pähkinöitä, sieniä, leipää ja leivonnaisia (joiden valmistamisessa ei ole käytetty eläinrasvaa tai maitotuotteita), muroja ja viljatuotteita jne.

Keittojen ja kastikkeiden tulee olla kasviperäisiä, eikä niissä saa olla liha- tai kanalientä. Ruoan valmistamisessa saa käyttää vain puhdasta kasviöljyä tai kasvimargariinia, mutta ei voita eikä muita eläinrasvoja.

Voisitteko tarjota vegaani aterian minulle/meille?

KIITOS

POUVEZ-VOUS LIRE CECI S'IL VOUS PLAÎT?

Je suis végan (végétalien(ne)) / Nous sommes végans

Par principe, les végans ne mangent aucun produit d'origine animale – dans l'intérêt des gens, des animaux et de l'environnement.

Donc nous ne mangeons pas: de viande (y compris hachis, saucisses, boudin), de volaille (y compris poulet), de poisson, de crustacés, coquillages ni fruits de mer; ni d'autres produits animaux tels que miel, oeufs, lait, beurre, fromage, et autres produits laitiers.

Mais nous mangeons: les pommes de terre, le riz, les pâtes (sans oeuf), les haricots, les légumes, les tomates, les fruits et fruits secs, les champignons; le pain et les pâtisseries faits sans matière grasse animale, sans oeufs, sans lait ni crème chantilly; les céréales et produits dérivés.

S'il vous plaît, proposez un repas en accord avec ce texte.

MERCI BEAUCOUP

Prégolle que lea esta información

Eu son vegano/eu son vegana
Nós somos veganos/nós somos veganas

Os que seguimos unha dieta vegana non consumimos produto ningún de orixe animal e mantemos unha postura ecoloxicamente responsable de respecto polos seres humanos, os animais e o medio ambiente.

Daquela, os veganos/veganas NON comemos: carne (incluida a carne picada e as sachichas), aves de curral (incluidos os polos), peixe, mariscos ou outros produtos coma o mel, os ovos, o leite, a manteiga, o queixo ou calquera outro produto lácteo.

Os veganos/veganas SI comemos: patacas, arroz, pastas alimenticias (sen ovo), legumes (xudías, garavanzos, lentellas, chícharos, etc), verduras, tomates, froita, froitos secos, sementes, cogumelos, pan ou pastelería (preparada sen ovo nin graxa animal), cereais e produtos a base de cereais ou de soia coma o tofu, etc.

As sopas e o prebe pódense facer con caldo vexetal, mais non con carne nin extracto de polo. Para cociñar debe utilizarse sempre aceite puro vexetal ou manteita pura vexetal e non a manteiga nin outra graxa animal ningunha.

GRAZAS POR PREPARAR A COMIDA SEGUNDO AS NOSAS NECESIDADES

BITTE BEACHTEN SIE FOLGENDE INFORMATIONEN

Ich ernähre mich/Wir ernähren uns vegan (rein pflanzlich)

Vegan lebende Menschen essen keine tierischen Lebensmittel, aus Verantwortung gegenüber Mensch, Tier und Umwelt.

Wir essen also kein: Fleisch (auch kein Hackfleisch, Wurst, Schinken, usw.), Geflügel (Hühnchen, Ente usw.) Fisch (auch keine Schalentiere wie Muscheln, Krabben usw.), noch andere Lebensmittel tierischer Herkunft wie Milchprodukte (Butter, Käse, Quark, Joghurt usw.), Eier, Schweineschmalz (noch andere tierische Fette) noch Honig.

Wir essen: Kartoffeln, Reis, Nudeln (ohne Eier), Erbsen, Bohnen u.a. Hülsenfrüchte, Gemüse, Tomaten, Obst, Nüsse, Pilze; Brot und Gebäck (ohne tiersche Fette hergestellt); Getreideprodukte, Sojaprodukte wie z.B. Tofu usw.

Verwenden Sie für Suppen und Sossen bitte Gemüsebrühe (keine Fleisch- bzw Hühnerbrühe). Zum Braten und Kochen bitte nur reines Pflanzenöl oder reine Pflanzenmargarine benutzen (keine Butter, Schmalz oder andere tierische Fette; Margarine ohne Zusatz von Sauermilch usw.).

Wir freuen uns sehr über eine unseren Wünschen entsprechende Mahlzeit.

VIELEN HERZLICHEN DANK

ΠΑΡΑΚΑΛΩ ΔΙΑΒΑΣΤΕ ΤΟ ΕΞΗΣ

Είμαι / είμαστε αυστηροί χορτοφάγοι (βήγαν).

Η αρχή των βήγαν (δηλαδή των αυστηρών χορτοφάγων) είναι να μην τρώνε ζωικά προϊόντα καθόλου, προς όφελος των ζώων, των ανθρώπων, και του περιβάλοντος.

ΔΕΝ ΤΡΩΜΕ: το κρέας (και φαγητά φτιαγμένα απο κρέας όπως μπιφτέκια, σουβλάκια, λουκανικά κλπ.), κοτόπουλα και άλλα πουλερικά, ψάρι και θαλασσινά (χταπόδι, οστρείδια, οστρακοϊδή κλπ.). Επίσης όλα τα άλλα ζωικά προϊόντα όπως μέλι, αυγά, γάλα, βούτυρο, τυρί, φετα, και τα άλλα γαλακτοκομικά προϊόντα.

Επαναλαμβάνω ότι δεν τρώμε καθόλου φαγητά που περιέχουν ζωικά προϊόντα.

ΤΡΩΜΕ: πατάτες, ρύζι, μακαρόνι (μην περιέχοντας αυγά), φασόλια, λαχανικά, ντομάτες, φρούτα, φυστίκια, μανιτάρια, ψωμί και ζυμαρικά φτιαχμένα χωρίς, ζωικά λιπαρά.

Τρώμε λαδερά μαγειρεμένα χωρίς ζωικά προϊόντα, φακές και φασολάδα, σαλάτες (χωρίς φέτα η μαγιονέζα) κλπ.

Οι σούπες και η σάλτσες δεν πρέπει να περιέχουν παράγοντα κρέατος η ζωικά λιπαρά Μόνο φυτικό λάδι η αγνή φυτική μαργαρίνη μπορεί να χρησιμοποιηθεί στο μαγείρεμα, όχι, όμως, το βούτυρο η άλλα ζωικά λιπαρά.

Παρακαλώ προμηθεύστε μας φαγητό σύμφωνα με τις απαιτήσεις μας.

ΕΥΧΑΡΙΣΤΩ ΠΟΛΥ

કૃપા કરીને આ વાંચશો

હું સંપૂર્ણ શાકાહારી છું / અને સંપૂર્ણ શાકાહારી ખાઈએ

અમારા સિદ્ધાંત પ્રમાણે સંપૂર્ણ શાકાહારી લોકો પ્રાણીઓમાંથી ઉત્પન્ન થયેલું કશું જ ખાય નહીં. — લોકોના, પ્રાણીઓના, તથા પર્યાવરણના કલ્યાણ માટે.

તેથી, અને આ વસ્તુઓ ખાતા નથી. —

માંસ (છોડવાનું પ્રાણીનું)

ઈંડા

ડૂધ કે ડૂધના પદાર્થો (ક્રીમ, દહીં, છાશ, માખણ, ઘી, ચીઝ......)

મધ

તથા આ વસ્તુઓના વાપરીને બનાવેલા છોડવાના પદાર્થો.

અમારાથી ન ખવાય વસ્તુઓના ઉદાહરણો —

• ડૂધમાંથી બનાવેલ મિઠાઈ જેવા કે : ડૂધપાક, બરફી, ખીર, શ્રીખંડ, માવાની મિઠાઈઓ (પેંડા, બરફી, ગુલાબજાંબુ) ચમનગુલ્લા વગેરે.

• માખણ ભાખેલી વસ્તુઓ (પાઈ-કાજ, સૅંડવિચ, માખણ વાળેલું ખૂબ......)

• પનીરના શાક, પકોડા, વગેરે..

• ડૂધની ચા, કોફી, ડૂધ કોકટેઈલ

• છાશ- દહીં વાપરીને બનાવેલી વસ્તુઓ (જલેબી, ઢોકળા, હાંડવો, ચેવલા, ખમણી, દહીંવડા, કઢી......)

• અમચૂર્ણ, કુલ્ફી, શિખરણ

• મિલ્ક ક્રીમ, ઈંડા અથવા માખણ વાપરીને બનાવેલ કેક, બિસ્કિટ,

• એમ કે બીજા વાપરીને કરેલ અલબત.

પણ વનસ્પતિમાંથી બનાવેલી પ્રત્યેક વસ્તુ અમને ચાલશે. જેવા કે —

ઘઉં, શાકભાજ, અનાજ, ડાળ, ફળો, કંદમૂળ, સૂકો મેવો, વગેરે....

અમારાથી પીવાય તેવા પીણાં —

શરબત (લિંબુ, કેરોમ, ડાળ જેવી....) ફળોના રસ, શ્રીફળની રસ, નળિયેર પાણી, ફળની ચા કે કોફી

અમારાથી ખાઈ શકાય એવી મિઠાઈઓ —

(શુદ્ધ ઘી ન વાપરી હોય તેવી..):

સુતરફેણી, આમ, લાડુ, ફેંસર, લાપસી, ગુલ્લાપાળી, બદ્વાર, શીરો........

નળવા માટે કે વધારામાં શુદ્ધ ઘી, માખણ વગેરે ન વાપરવા. ઉલટ વનસ્પતિ ઘી કે તેલ વાપરવા.

ગાંઠિનો વરખ લગાડેલા ઠીઠ્યાના વસ્તુ ચાલશે નહીં.

કૃપા કરીને અમને અમારી જરૂરિયાતી જણવતું ભોજન આપશો.

આભાર ! ધન્યવાદ !

נא לקרוא את הדף הזה

אני טבעוני / אני טבעונית / אנו טבעונים

באופן עקרוני, טבעונים אינם אוכלים שום דבר מן החי -
לטובת בני אדם, בעלי חיים ואיכות הסביבה.

כלומר, איננו אוכלים:

בשר (כולל בשר טחון, נקניקיות וכו'), עוף, דגים, מאכלי-
ים (ביצי דגים/שרימפס/קלאמרי וכו'), או מוצרים אחרים
מן החי כגון דבש, ביצים, חלב, חמאה, גבינה או דברי-
חלב אחרים (גם לא אבקות חלב).

אך אנו כן אוכלים:

תפוחי-אדמה, אורז, פסטות (ללא ביצים), קטניות
ושעועית, ירקות, עגבניות, פירות, אגוזים, פטריות, לחמים
ודברי-מאפה ללא שומן מן החי וללא ביצים, דגנים וכו'.
אנו אוכלים מרקים ללא אבקות מן החי (בלי "אבקת
מרק בשרית") וללא צירי בשר או עוף. מותר להשתמש
בבישול רק בשמן צמחי או מרגרינה צמחית טהורה, לא
חמאה או כל שומן אחר מן החי.

האם באפשרותך להכין ארוחה שתענה על צרכינו?

תודה רבה

कृपया इसे पढ़ें

मैं सम्पूर्ण शाकाहारी हूँ / हम सम्पूर्ण शाकाहारी हैं

सिद्धान्त से, हम सम्पूर्ण शाकाहारी व्यक्ति पशुओं से बनी/निकाली गयी कोई भी वस्तु नहीं खाते—मनुष्य, पशु तथा पर्यावरण के हित के लिये।

इसलिये, हम यह वस्तुएँ नहीं खाते—

मांस (किसी भी पशु, पक्षी, या मछली का), अण्डे, दूध तथा दुग्ध पदार्थ (जैसे मलाई, दही, मट्ठा, मक्खन, चीज़, घ ...) शहद, और इन वस्तुओं से बना कोई पदार्थ भी।

इन्हें न चलनेवाले पदार्थों के उदाहरण—

- दूध से बनी मिठाइयाँ : गुलाब जामुन, पेड़ा, बर्फी, रसगुल्ला, खीर, असली घी से बना हलवा, लड्डू, ...
- मक्खन के पदार्थ : पाव-भाजी, सैंडविच, मक्खन डले हुए सूप या शोरबे, ...
- पनीर की सब्ज़ियों/परॉंठे/पकोड़े
- दही-मट्ठे से बनाए पदार्थ : दही-वड़ा, कढ़ी, लस्सी, दही की चटनियों; रायते, ...
- आईस-क्रीम, कुल्फी, मिल्क-शेक, दूध की चाय/कॉफ़ी
- मिल्क-ब्रेड; अण्डे/मक्खन/दूध डले हुए चॉकलेट, केक, और बिस्किट

परन्तु हमें वनस्पति-विश्व की सब वस्तुएँ स्वीकार हैं,
जैसे फल, सब्ज़ियों, अनाज, दालें, इत्यादि।

हमें चलनेवाले पेय—
नीम्बू का शर्बत, फलों का रस, गन्ने का रस, नारियल का पानी, काली चाय/कॉफ़ी

हमें चलनेवाली मिठाइयाँ—
असली घी न डला हुआ हलवा, लड्डू, रेवड़ी, ...

- ★ तलने के लिये या छौंक(तड़का) में केवल वनस्पति तेलों का उपयोग करें, असली घी या मक्खन का नहीं
- ★ किसीभी वस्तु पर चान्दी का वर्क न लगा हो।
- ★ किसीभी पदार्थ पर मलाई/चीज़/मक्खन की सजावट न हो।

कृपया हमारे सिद्धान्तों और आहारनियमों के अनुसार हमें भोजन दें।   धन्यवाद

KÉREM, OLVASSA EL

Vegán vagyok / Vegánok vagyunk

A *vegánok* elvből nem esznek semmilyen állati eredetű terméket az emberek, állatok és a természet érdekében.

Igy nem eszünk: húst (beleértve a darált húst, kolbászt és egyebet), baromfit (csirkét sem), halat, kagylót vagy egyéb állati terméket, mint például mézet, tojást, tejet, vajat, sajtot vagy más egyéb tejterméket.

Viszont eszünk: krumplit, rizst, tésztát (tojás nélkül), babot, zöldséget, paradicsomot, gyümölcsöt, diót, gombát, állati zsiradék nélkül készült pékárút és süteményeket, gabonaféléket és ebböl készült termékeket és igy tovább.

Levesek és mártások készíthetők zöldségalapból hús vagy baromfiszármazék nélkül. A főzéshez tiszta zöldségolajat vagy tiszta zöldségmargarint lehet használni, de vajat vagy állati zsiradékot nem.

Kérem, készítsenek olyan ételeket, amelyek ezen elvárásaink szerint készülnek.

KÖSZÖNÖM SZÉPEN

VINSAMLEGAST LESIÐ ÞETTA

Ég er urtingi / við erum urtingjar

Orðið urtingi (algrænmetisæti, strangur grænmetisæti) er notað fyrir þá sem af grunnvallarsjónarmiðum borða ekki neitt úr dýraríkinu, vegna umhyggju um manneskjur, dýr og umhverfi.

Þessvegna borðum við ekki: kjöt (þar með talið hakkað kjöt, pylsur o sv frv), kjúkling, fisk, skeldýr, hrogn/kavíar eða aðrar framleiðsluvörur úr dýraríkinu eins og hunang, egg, mjólk, skyr, smjör, ost eða aðrar mjólkurvörur.

En við borðum: kartöflur, hrís, pasta, baunir, grænmeti, tómötur/rauðaldin, ávexti, hnetur, sveppa, brauð eða kökur án fits úr dýraríkinu, korn og vörur framleiddar úr korni o sv frv.

Súpur og sósur má búa til úr grænmetissoði en ekki úr kjöt- eða kjúklingasoði. Til matreiðslu má nóta jurtaolíu eða hreint mjólkurlaust smjörlíki, ekki smjör, mör eða annað fit úr dýraríkinu.

Vinsamlegast gerið svo vel að búa til máltíð samkvæmt óskum okkar!

KÆRAR ÞAKKIR!

SILAHKAN BACA DENGAN TELITI

Saya adalah seorang Vegan / Kami adalah Vegan atau Murni Vegetarian

Pada prinsipnya, seorang "vegan" tidak memakan makanan yang berasal dari hewan/binatang – untuk kepentingan makhluk hidup seperti manusia, hewan dan lingkungan.

Oleh karena itu, kami tidak makan: daging (termasuk daging yang dicincang halus), binatang ternak (termasuk ayam, itik, angsa, arnab, babi, sapi, kambing dan sebagainya) ikan, udang, kepiting, kerang dan makanan yang berasal dari hewan atau serangga seperti madu, telur, susu, mentega, keju dan semua makanan yang mengandung susu/telur.

Tetapi kami makan: kentang, beras, gamdum, 'pasta' (tidak mengandung telur), kacang, sayur-sayuran, tomat, buah-buahan, biji-bijian, jamur, roti atau kue yang tidak mengandung minyak atau lemak hewan, ubi-ubian, jagung dan sebagainya.

Kuah, untuk sop atau dibuat dari bahan sayur-sayuran / tumbuh-tumbuhan tetapi tidak menggunakan daging atau ayam. Hanya minyak atau mentega yang terbuat dari sayur-sayuran murni yang boleh digunakan dalam masakan kami. Minyak, lemak atau mentega yang terbuat dari hewan tidak boleh digunakan.

Silahkan dan tolong sediakan makanan yang memenuhi permintaan kami diatas.

TERIMA KASIH

Is vegan mé
(feoilséantóir amach is amach).

Ciallaíonn sé sin: Dé réir mo phrionsabal ní ithim rud ar bith de bhunús ainmhí.

Dá bhrí sin ní ithim: feoil, iasc, cloicheáin, diúilicíní, éanlaithe, nó feoil eile mar ispíní 'rl. Freisin ní ólaim bainne, agus ní ithim cáis, uibheacha, nó táirgí bainne.

Ithim: glasraí, prátaí, trátaí, cnóanna, beacáin, rís, torthaí, grán agus grántáirgí 'rl.

Ithim anraithí, anlanna 'rl (fhad is nach bhfuil siad insilithe d'fheoil nó d'éanlaithe nó a leithéid), ach tá anraithí agus anlanna as glasraí ceadaithe.

Caithfidh bia bheith bácáilte nó róstaithe in ola fíorphlandiúl nó margairín, ach ní in uachtar ime nó in aon saill ainmhí.

PER CORTESIA, LE DISPIACEREBBE LEGGER CIÒ CHE SEGUE?

Io sono vegano / Noi siamo vegani.

Per principio, i vegani non si nutrono di nessun prodotto di origine animale, in modo che ne possano trarre beneficio persone, animali e l'ambiente.

Di conseguenza, noi non mangiamo: carne (tritata, salsiccia, salame, prosciutto, ecc.), pollame (compresa ogni tipo di selvaggina in genere), pesce, molluschi ed altri prodotti di origine animale quali miele, uova, latte, burro, formaggio, e prodotti derivati dal latte.

Ma contrario noi mangiamo: patate, riso, pasta (senza uova), fagioli, ortaggi, pomodori, frutta, nocciole, mandorle e frutti simili, funghi; pane o dolci prodotti senza utilizzare grassi di origine animale; cereali e derivati, ecc.

Zuppe, minestre, passati e salse possono essere preparate utilizzando dadi di origine vegetale senza estratti di carne di ogni tipo. Per la cottura si possono utilizzare olii o margarine vegetali, ma non burro e altri grassi di origine animale (es. strutto).

Per cortesia, potete prepararci dei pasti che siano compatibili con le nostre esigenze?

GRAZIE

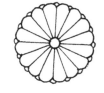

これを読んでください

私（私たち）は完全菜食主義者（ビーガン）です。

主義として、人間、動物、環境のために動物性のものは
一切食べません。

そのため、以下のものは食べません：
肉類（ひき肉、ハム、ソーセージ、ベーコン、鳥肉等を含む）魚介類、そして
動物性製品である蜂蜜、卵、牛乳、バター、チーズなどの乳製品など。

しかし以下のものは食べます：
野菜（トマト、白菜類、キノコ類、芋類など）海草、果物、豆類、ナッツ類、
穀物（動物性脂肪、卵を含まないパンとめん類、米、麦類、コーンフレイクな
ど）。

スープやソースは肉エキスではなく野菜からできているものだけに限ります。
動物性脂肪やバターではなく、純粋な植物油や、純粋に植物のみからできてい
るマーガリンを使用したものに限ります。

どうぞ私（たち）の要望に沿った料理を作って下さい。

ご協力を心より感謝します！

ದಯವಿಟ್ಟು ಇದನ್ನು ಓದಿರಿ

ನಾನು ಅಹಿಂಸಾಹಾರಿ (ವೀಗನ್–ಸಂಪೂರ್ಣ ಸಸ್ಯಾಹಾರಿ)/
ನಾವು ಅಹಿಂಸಾಹಾರಿಗಳು (ವೀಗನ್ ಗಳು–ಸಂಪೂರ್ಣ ಸಸ್ಯಾಹಾರಿಗಳು)

ಅಹಿಂಸಾಹಾರಿಗಳು, ಸಿದ್ಧಾಂತದ ಆಧಾರದ ಮೇಲೆ, ಮಾನವರ, ಪ್ರಾಣಿಗಳ ಮತ್ತು ಪರಿಸರದ ಒಳಿತಿಗಾಗಿ, ಪ್ರಾಣಿಮೂಲದ ಯಾವುದೇ ವಸ್ತುಗಳನ್ನು ಸೇವಿಸುವುದಿಲ್ಲ.

ಆದ್ದರಿಂದ, ನಾವು ಇವುಗಳನ್ನು ತಿನ್ನುವುದಿಲ್ಲ:
ಯಾವುದೇ ಪ್ರಾಣಿ, ಪಕ್ಷಿ ಅಥವಾ ಮೀನಿನಿಂದ ಪಡೆದ ಮಾಂಸ, ಮೊಟ್ಟೆ, ಹಾಲು, ಮೊಸರು, ಮಜ್ಜಿಗೆ, ಬೆಣ್ಣೆ, ತುಪ್ಪ, ಗಿಣ್ಣು, ಖೋವಾ(ಪನ್ನೀರ್), ಜೇನು ಮೊದಲಾದ ಪ್ರಾಣಿಮೂಲದ ವಸ್ತುಗಳು ಮತ್ತು ಅವುಗಳನ್ನು ಬೆರೆಸಿ ತಯಾರಿಸಿದ ಮೊಸರನ್ನ, ಜಾಮೂನ್, ಪೇಡ ಮೊದಲಾದ ಆಹಾರಗಳು.

ಆದರೆ ಇವುಗಳನ್ನು ತಿನ್ನುತ್ತೇವೆ:
ಅಕ್ಕಿ, ಗೋಧಿ, ಜೋಳ, ಎಲ್ಲಾ ವಿಧದ ತರಕಾರಿಗಳು, ಹಣ್ಣುಗಳು, ಬೇಳೆ–ಕಾಳುಗಳು, ಎಣ್ಣೆ, ವನಸ್ಪತಿ ಮುಂತಾದ ಸಂಪೂರ್ಣ ಸಸ್ಯಾಹಾರಿ ವಸ್ತುಗಳು ಮತ್ತು ಯಾವುದೇ ಪ್ರಾಣಿಮೂಲದ ವಸ್ತುಗಳನ್ನು ಉಪಯೋಗಿಸದೇ ತಯಾರಿಸಲಾದ ಇಡ್ಲಿ, ವಡೆ, ಚಪಾತಿ, ದೋಸೆ, ಮೊದಲಾದ ಆಹಾರಗಳು.

ದಯವಿಟ್ಟು ನಮ್ಮ ಈ ಆಹಾರ ನಿಯಮಕ್ಕೆ ಸರಿಹೊಂದುವ ಆಹಾರವನ್ನು ಕೊಡಬಹುದೇ?.

ಕೃತಜ್ಞತೆಗಳು!

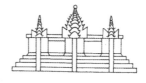

គំនូសបញ្ឈរបាត /ឬពាក៍ ប៉ ប៉ ប៉ បង្ហាញនេះ:ទេ
ព្យាកឃើញម៉ងំបញ្ឈរ /បងជួបពាក់តាមថ់ាំងនេះ:ទេ,
ឬឬហ៊ាន តាច់ថ្មា, តាច់ក្រោ តាច់ឋាន់ តាច់ត្រី
ថ៍/ប្រស្បាក់ ។ និងតតនិតតស្បៀ។ ១៦១ ក្នុង។
ទំងុប, តិត, ទំងេេះ:ទេ, បរំ, ឃើត នីង
រប៉ត/និងតតនិត េេ៍ត់ទំកេះ:គេ.
ប៉ត់ព្យាកឃើងកាចបបំពោតវបប៉តំាងនេះ:បាន
ត្តិចង នីឃ្នស ក្ហាយ តត្ឃេក បចិត បេំងផ៊ុ
នៃនតេ ក្របាឃាយចន់ ផ្ញុត, ថ៍ន៉ូងំនតនាបិន
ក្ហានេថ្មីនីឃ្នួយតាច់េេឃបនំាព្ញាញា
លឃ្ម ក្ហាបំន៉ំនទំតិតេេះ: នីឃតឃនេំនិឃ្នួយម៉បិន
តាបបម៉ាចាតក្ហា, បេ៍ថ្មីត៍តាច់ម៉ម៉ំរកាច
ប៉ំចាតបាន ។ ក្ហាបច៍ំនិឃ្ញួយឃ១ឃបតំ
ចាច្ញាបាន ថ៉ំនំប៉ំនិឃ្ញួយថ៍ំ ។ ញាញាតត
មិន ចាច្ញាបាន.

ក្ហ៊ុបលាយក៍ឃាយ៍និឍ ក្រ៍តំលឃ។

Kripia hem matxe dian divun vachat →

Hanv/ami xivraki

Nema pormonnem xiuraki monzati thaun utpon zata titlelm bilkul khaina; karann monxea, monzati ani amchea vatavoronna borea pasot.

Mhonnttoch hantiem ami kainch khaina

mas – khimo, cherusam adi; vho poltry jem utpon korta; zoxem kombio, nustem, khoitem axil'lem nustem vho dusre koslei monzatichem utpadan zoxem mhony, tantiam, dud, mosko, paneer ani her dudachem utpadan zal'lem.

Punn hem ami khatanu

bhottatte, tandul, pasta punn tantiam nasul'lem, dapichem kaddan vho chonne, torkari, tomatt, follam biknna, almem, khott'tem axil'lem foll, unddo, maideachea pittachim khanna - zoxem biscutt, kek punn – monzatichi chorob nastana; annad hania ani tachem utpadan, adi., kald, sos (ruch hadpi chettni) torkarechea bandavalan kel'lem foki, punn mas vho khoincheai masacho pillun kaddlolo ros bilkul ghalunk xokona. Fokot xud'dh torkarechem tel, vho pav (moskea bhaxen ros margerine), jevonn randta tedna vaprunk xokta. Punn mosko vho kosleai zonvarachi vos vaprunkzaina.

Kripia, amche gorjek upkarta toslem jevonn amkam mellum xem korat.

아래 요청을 들어 주십시오

우리는 "베이건" 입니다

원 칙 적으로, 베이건들은 동물성 음식을 - 인류와,
짐승들과, 환경을 위하여 - 절대로 먹지 않습니다.

그럼으로, 우리는 각종 육류 (소세지나, 곱창, 순대 같이
가공된 육류를 포함하여), 각종 새고기 (닭 ,오리, 꿩
고기등), 모든 어산물 (물고기, 조개, 젓갈, 생선 알,등)
및 기타 동물성 음식물 (꿀, 각종 알, 우유, 버터, 치즈,
요구르트를 비롯한 우유및 양유의 가공품) 등을 먹지
않습니다.

그러나, 우리는 모든 식물성 음식; 각종 곡류 (쌀, 보리,
밀, 콩, 옥수수, 등), 야채, 산채 (나물, 고사리, 버섯)라
그 가공물 (두부, 국수, 빵) 등을, 동물성 기름으로
조리하지 않았을 경우 얼마든지 먹습니다.

국이나 양념들도, 야채로 만든 경우는 괜찮지만, 동물성
고기나, 생선, 혹은 닭고기로 만든 국은 먹지 않습니다.
요리할때는, 순 식물성 기름 (참기름, 콩기름)이나, 식물성
마가린 만 시용하며, 동물성 기름 (버터, 돼지기름, 소기름)
은 절대로 쓰지 않습니다.

죄송 하지만, 거희에게 위 조건에 맞는 음식을 제공해
주시면 매우 고맙 겠습 니다.

໖- ຊ) ເບິ່ງຮູບພາບ.

ພາງໂທລະໂຄ : ຊຸບພາບເຫລົ່ານີ້ເປັນຫຍັງ ບຸນທາດຫລວງເວຽງຈັນ.

ເດັກນ້ອຍ : ມັນ (ຊ) ແກະສະລັກເປັນແບບໃດ...) ນັ້ນ,
ໂທລະ (ຄອນ) ແມ່ນ...

'ເຄື່ອງ...'.

ນາຍຄູ : ຄຳ,ຖາມ,ເວົ້າ,ຖາມ,ຄິດ,ເວົ້າ,ພາກຫລາຍ,ແລະ

ພາກໂທ ບຸນພາບພາບ ແລະ

'ຄິດ','ຄວາມ','ຈັນ','ບໍ'.

Es esmu stingrs veìetârietis (e)

Mçs esam stingri veìetârieði

Principiâli stingri veìetârieði neçd dzîvnieku izcelðanas çdienus – tas ir par labu cilvçkiem, dzîvniekiem un apkârtçjai videi.

Tâ kâ mçs neçdam: gaïu (iekïaujot malto gaïu, cîsiòus utt.), putnu gaïu (iekïaujot vistas gaïu), zivis, vçþveidîgus vai citus dzîvnieku produktus, tâdus kâ medu, olas, pienu, sviestu, sieru vai citus piena produktus.

Bet mçs çdam: kartupeïus, rîsus, makaronus (kas nesatur olas), pupinas, dârzeòus, tomâtus, augïus, riekstus, sçnes; konditorejas izstrâdâjumus, kas nesatur dzîvnieku taukus; labîbas augus un labîbas produktus utt.

Zupas un mçrces var bût izgatavotas uz dârzeòu pamata, bet bez ekstraktiem no gaïas vai vistas. Cepðanas procesâ var lietot tikai tîru dârzeòu eïïu vai tîru dârzeòu margarînu, bez sviesta vai kâdiem citiem dzîvnieku taukiem.

Vai jûs varçtu, lûdzu, pagatavot çdienu, kas atbilstu mûsu prasîbâm?

LIELS PALDIES JUMS!

PRAÐAU PERSKAITYK ÐITAI

Að esu veganas/mes esame veganai

Veganai nevalgo visko, kas yra gyvûninës kilmës, nes tai naudinga þmonëms, gyvûnams ir aplinkai.

Taigi, mes nevalgom: mësos (áskaitant farðà, deðreles ir pan.), paukðtienos (áskaitant viðtienà), þuvies, vëþiagyviø ir kitø gyvûninës kilmës produktø, tokiø kaip medus, kiauðiniai, pienas, sviestas, sûris ir kiti pieno produktai.

Taèiau mes valgom: makaronus (kurie pagaminti nenaudojant kiauðiniø), bulves, ryþius, pupeles, pomidorus ir kitas darþoves, vaisius, rieðutus, grybus, grûdus ir grûdø produktus, duonà ir pyragus, pagamintus be gyvûniniø riebalø. Sriubos ir padaþai gali bûti pagaminti ið darþoviø, taèiau be gyvûninës kilmës ingredientø.

Tik grynas augalinis aliejus ir grynas augalinis margarinas gali bûti naudojami gaminant valgá, bet tik ne sviestas ar kiti gyvûniniai riebalai.

Ar galëtum paruoðti maistà, kuris atitinka mûsø reikalavimus?

AÈIÛ TAU LABAI

Mivelona amin'ny zava-maniry aho.

Ny dikany dia izao: araka ny foto-kevitro dia tsy minihan-javatra avy amin'ny biby aho. Toy ny hena, trondro, patsabe, bibin-drano-masina, vorona (akoho) na ny hafa, ohatra: totokena, saosiny, sns. Kanefa koa ny ronono, fromazy, atody, na karazan-dronono hafa.

Eny mihinana ny karazan'anana aho, ovy, voatabia, voanio, holatra, vary, voankazo, voa maina, na zxavatra avy amin'ny voa maina; sns.

Ny lasopy, ny lasaosy, sy ny hafa kosa dia tsy andrahona amin'ny hena, henamborona, sy ny toy izany, fa kosa amin'ny karazan'anana. Manao mofo na manendy sakafo amin'ny tena menaka fanendasana ihany na amin'ny margarinu, fa tsy amin'ny herotra dibera na amin'ny menaka avy amin'ny biby hafa.

**Saya seorang 'vegan' atau 'vegetarian' sepenuh /
kami 'vegan' atau 'vegetarian' sepenuh**

Pada asasnya, seorang "vegan" tidak makan makanan yang berasal dari haiwan/binatang - bagi faedah manusia, haiwan dan alam semulajadi.

Sebab itu, kami tidak makan: daging (termasuk daging yang dicincang halus), binatang ternakan (termasuk ayam, itik, angsa, arnab, babi, lembu, kambing dan sebagainya) ikan, ketam, udang, tiram, dan makanan yang berasal dari haiwan atau serangga seperti madu, telur, susu, mentega, keju dan hasil tenusu yang lain.

Tetapi kami makan: kentang, beras, gamdum, 'pasta' (tidak mengandungi telur), kacang, sayur-sayuran, tomato, buah-buahan, buah bijiran, cendawan, roti atau kuih yang tidak mengandungi minyak atau lemak haiwan, makanan bijiran dan sebaginya.

Kuah, sos dan gulai yang dibuat daripada sayur-sayuran / tumbuh-tumbuhan tetapi tidak menggunakan hasil daging dan sebagainya. Hanya minyak atau mentega sayur-sayuran yang tulen boleh digunakan dalam masakan kami. Minyak, lemak atau mentega haiwan tidak boleh digunakan.

Sila sedikan makanan yang memenuhi kehendak kami.

TERIMA KASIH

ദയവുചെയ്ത് ഇത് വായിക്കുക

ഞാൻ പരിശുദ്ധ സസ്യാഹാരി.
ഞങ്ങൾ പരിശുദ്ധ സസ്യാഹാരികൾ

താത്വികമായി സസ്യാഹാരികൾ മൃഗങ്ങളിൽനിന്ന് ലഭിക്കുന്ന യാതൊന്നും കഴിക്കുകയില്ല. പരിതസ്ഥിതിക്കും ജനങ്ങളുടെ നന്മയ്ക്കുംവേണ്ടി.

ഇവകൾ ഭക്ഷിക്കുന്നില്ല.
ഇക്കാരണങ്ങളാൽ ഞങ്ങൾ മൃഗങ്ങളിൽനിന്നും ലഭിക്കുന്ന മാംസം, മുട്ട, മത്സ്യം എന്നിവയും പ്രാണികളിൽനിന്ന് ലഭിക്കുന്ന തേൻ, പാൽ എന്നിവ യും കഴിക്കുകയില്ല.

ഇവകൾ ഭക്ഷിക്കുന്നു.
ഞങ്ങൾ ഉരുളക്കിഴങ്ങ്, അരി, ബീൻസ്, പച്ചക്കറികൾ പഴം, കൂൺ, ബദാംപിസ്ത തുടങ്ങിയവ, പരിപ്പ് വർഗ്ഗങ്ങൾ എന്നിവ കഴിക്കുന്നു.
പച്ചക്കറികളിൽനിന്ന് ഉണ്ടാക്കിയ സൂപ്പ് പരിശുദ്ധമായ എണ്ണകൾ എന്നിവ മാത്രം ഉപയോഗിക്കുന്നു.

ഈ തത്വങ്ങൾക്ക് അനുസരിച്ച ആഹാരം ഉണ്ടാക്കാൻ കഴിയുമോ?

താങ്കൾക്ക് നന്ദി.

Jiena Vegan,

Għalhekk fuq prinċipji ta' ħarsien ta' l-ambjent, l-annimali u għal benfiċċju tal-bnedmin, jien la niekol laħam u l-ebda prodott li jiġi mill-annimali.

Jiena ma nikolx: laħam, (inkluż kapuljat, kull kwalità ta'zalzett eċċ), tjur (inkluż tiġieġ), ħut, gambli, maskli, jew prodotti oħra li jiġu mill-annimali bħal għasel, bajd, ħalib, butir, ġobon u prodotti oħra magħmulin mill-ħalib.

Iżda jiena niekol: patata, ross, għaġin (mhux magħmul mill-bajd) fażola, ħaxix, tadam, frott, lewż, faqqiegħ, ħobż, pasti mhux magħmula mix-xaħam ta' l-annimali, ċereali u prodotti magħmula miċ-ċereali eċċ.

Sopop u zlazi jistgħu jsiru bi stokk tal-ħaxix, iżda mhux bl-estratt la tal-laħam ,la tat-tiġieġ u lanqas tal-ħut. Fit-tisjir jista' jintuża biss żejt tal-ħaxix, jew marġerina magħmula mill-ħaxix u mhux butir jew xaħam tal-annimali.

Jekk jogħġbok tista' tipprovdilna ikla skond il-ħtiġijiet tagħna?

Grazzi ħafna.

कृपया हे वाचा

मी सम्पूर्ण शाकाहारी आहे / आम्ही सम्पूर्ण शाकाहारी आहोत

सिद्धान्ता प्रमाणे, आम्ही सम्पूर्ण शाकाहारी व्यक्ति प्राण्यांपासून बनविलेल्या/काढलेल्या कुठल्याहि वस्तु खात नाही—मनुष्य, पशु, व पर्यावरणाच्या हितासाठी.

म्हणून, आम्ही ह्या गोष्टी खात नाही—

मांस (कुठल्याहि प्राण्याचे—पशु, पक्षी, मासे, ...), अण्डी, दूध व दुधाचे पदार्थ (साय, दही, ताक, लोणी, चीझ, तूप ...), मध, व ह्या गोष्टी आसलेले कुठलेहि पदार्थ सुद्धा.

आम्हाला न चालणाऱ्या गोष्टींची उदाहरणे—

- दुधापासून बनविलेली मिष्टान्ने : श्रीखण्ड, दूध-पाक, बासुन्दी, गुलाब-जामुन, पेढा, ...
- लोणी/तूप असलेले पदार्थ : पाव-भाजी, सँडविच, साजुक तुपात बनविलेला शिरा, लाडू, वड्या, ...
- पनीर च्या भाज्या/पराठे/पकोडे
- ताक-दह्याचे पदार्थ : दही-वडा, कढी, लस्सी, दह्यातल्या चटण्या/कोशिम्बिरी, ढोकळा, सुरळीची वडी, ...
- आईस-क्रीम, कुल्फी, मिल्क-शेक, दुधाचा चहा/कॉफी
- मिल्क-ब्रेड; अण्डा/लोणी/दूध असलेले चॉकलेट, केक, व बिस्किट

पण आम्हाला वनस्पति-विश्वातल्या सर्व गोष्टी चालण्या सारख्या आहेत.
जसे फळे, भाज्या, अन्न, डाळी, कन्द-मुळे, सुका मेवा, इत्यादि.

आम्हाला चालणारी पेये—
सरबत (लिम्बू, कोकम, पन्हे, ...), फळांचा/उसाचा रस, नारळाचे पाणी, कोरा चहा/कॉफी

आम्हाला चालणारी मिष्टान्ने—
(कश्यालाहि साजुक तूप न लावलेले) :
पुरण पोळी, गुळाची पोळी, नारळी भात, शिरा, लाडू, चिरोटा, करंजी, मोदक, ...

- ★ तळायला व फ्रोडणी साठी साजुक तूप किंवा लोणी न वापरता केवळ वनस्पति तेले वापरावीत.
- ★ कुठल्याही पदार्थांवर चान्दीचा वर्ख लावलेला नसावा.
- ★ वरुन साय (क्रीम), चीझ, लोणी वगैरेंची सजावट नसावी.

कृपया आमच्या आहारनियमांनुसार आम्हाला जेवण पुरवा. आभारी आहोत

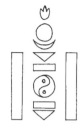

Би веган гэдэг ургамлаар хоологч.

Миний итгэх байгаа бол би амьтны биеэс гарсан нэг ч иддэггүй гэж байна.

Тийм учраас би мах, татсан мах, янз бурийн хиам, загас, сам хорхой хяcaa, янз бурийн идзж болох шувуу тахиа гэх мэт, суу, бяслаг, өндөг, янх бурийн цагаан идээ иддэггүй гэж байна.

Гэвч би идэшний ногоо, төмс, лооль, самар, мөөг, цагаан будаа, жимс, эрдэнэ шиш, эрдэнэ шишээр хийсэн олон янзын идэш иддэг.

Шөл, сумс бол заавал чанасан идэшний ногооны шимээр хийх ёстой байна. Шөл, сумс нь мах, тахианы шимээр хийх болхгүй.

Би ургамлын тос, ургамлын урийн тос, ургамлын маргарин тосоор шарсан ба хайрсан хоол иддэг. Би цөцгийн тос, малын өөхөөр шарсан хайрсан хоол иддэггүй.

कृपया यो पढ्नुहोस्

म साकाहारी हुँ । हामी साकाहारी हौँ

सिद्धान्ततः भेगानहरूले मानिसहरू, पशुहरू र
गतावरणको लागि पशुबाट उत्पादित खानेकुरा
कैही पनि खाँदैनन् ।

यसकारण हामी खाँदैनौ :-
मासु (धुलो बनास्को मासु अथवा किमा र ससेज),
कुरुरा, माछा, सिपीबाछा अथवा अरू पशुबाट उत्पादित
जस्तै मह, अण्डा, नौनी, चिज अथवा अरू दूधबाट
बनेको खानेकुराहरू ।
तर हामी खाहछौँ :
आलु, भात, अण्डाबिनाको पास्ता, गेगगुडी, सागसब्जी,
गोलभेडा, फलफूल, सुपारी, च्याउ, पशुको घ्यूबिना
बनेको रोटी र पास्ट्री ; खाद्य अन्न इत्यादि ।

कृपया हामीले भनेजस्तो खुटा खाना बनाउन
संम्भर छ कि ?

धेरै धेरै धन्यवाद

VENNLIGST LES DETTE:

Jeg er veganer / vi er veganere

Veganere spiser av prinsipp ikke noe av animalsk opphav, av hensyn til mennesker, dyr og miljø.

Så vi spiser ikke: kjøtt (inkl. kjøttdeig, pølser, etc.), fjærkre (inkl. kylling), fisk, skalldyr, eller andre animalske produkter slik som honning, egg, melk, smør, ost og andre meieriprodukter.

Men vi spiser: poteter, ris, pasta (uten egg), bønner, grønnsaker, tomater, frukt, nøtter, sopp, brød og bakeriprodukter uten animalsk fett, korn og kornprodukter, etc.

Supper og sauser kan lages med vegetabilsk buljong, men uten kjøtt- eller kyllingekstrakt. Kun ren vegetabilsk olje eller rent plantemargarin kan brukes til steking, hverken smør eller noe annet slags animalsk fett.

Vennligst skaff oss et måltid sam tilfredsstiller våre krav.

TUSEN TAKK

لطفاً این را بخوانید

من یک گیاهخوار هستم / ما گیاهخوار هستیم

اصولاً و بطور کلی گیاهخواران هیچگونه مواد غذائی که اصلش را بمنشاء آن حیوانی
باشد استفاده نخواهند کرد و دلیل این امر هم خاطر فوائد و مزایائی است که گیاهخواری
برای مردم ، حیوانات ، محیط زیست و طبیعت دارد میباشد .

بنابراین ما زاین غذاها پرهیز میکنیم :
گوشت (بهمین فرآورده های گوشتی جون کالباس ، ژامبون و غیره) گوشت پرندگان
(مرغ) ماهی ، صدف ، همینطور تولیدات حیوانی جون عسل ، تخم مرغ ، شیر ، کره ،
پنیر و سایر لبنیات .
ولی ازاین غذاها استفاده میکنیم :
سیب زمینی ، برنج ، اسپاگتی و ماکارونی (بدون تخم مرغ) ، لوبیا ، سبزیجات ، سبزیجات
گوجه فرنگی ، میوه جات ، دانه های روغنی ، تخمه جات ، تماچ جات ، نان ، کره گیاهی ، فندق ، پسته
و مانند آنها ، حبوبات ، شیرینی جات که بدون چربی و مواد حیوانی تهیه شده باشد ، غلات
و غیره .
سوپ ها و سس هائی که منشاء و مایه اصلی آنها گیاهی باشد نه آنکه منشاء آنها از گوشت
حیوانات و یا گوشت مرغ باشد .   فقط از روغن های خالص گیاهی و یا روغن نباتی خالص
را میتوان پخت و پز استفاده کرد دیگر و یا چربی های حیوانی نمیتوان استفاده کرد .

لطفاً یک نوع غذای مطلوب و باب طبع با خواسته های ما باشد تهیه و آماده نمائید .

سپاسگزارم

PROSZĘ TO PRZECZYTAĆ

**Jestem weganinem / Jestem weganką /
Jesteśmy weganinami / Jesteśmy wegankami.**

Weganie z zasady, kierując się dobrem ludzi, zwierząt i środowiska, nie jedzą żadnych pokarmów pochodzenia zwierzęcego.

Nasze pożywienie nie zawiera: mięsa (wędlin, mielonego, itd.), drobiu (w tym kurcząt), ryb, skorupiaków, ani innych produktów pochodzenia zwierzęcego, takich jak miód, jajka, mleko, masło, sery, i inne produkty mleczne.

Na nasze pożywienie składają się: ziemniaki, ryż, makaron bezjajeczny, groch, fasola, warzywa, pomidory, owoce, orzechy, nasiona, grzyby, pieczywo, zwykłe i słodkie nie zawierające jajek, mleka i tłuszczu zwierzęcego oraz kasze i mak.

Zupy i sosy powinny być przygotowane na wywarze warzywnym i nie mogą zawierać wywarów lub koncentratów mięsnych czy drobiowych. Do przygotowywania potraw należy używać czysty olej roślinny lub margarynę wyprodukowaną wyłącznie z olejów roślinnych, nie stosować masła ani innych tł uszczów pochodzenia zwierzęcego.

Prosimy o pożywienie, które spełnia nasze wymagania.

DZIĘKUJĘ / DZIĘKUJEMY

POR FAVOR LEIA ISTO

**Eu sou vegan / Nós somos vegans
(vegetarianos puros)**

Por princípio, nós não comemos nenhum produto de origem animal - para benefício das pessoas, dos animais, e do meio ambiente.

Assim sendo nós não comemos: carne (incluindo carne moída, salsichas, etc.), aves domésticas (incluindo frango), peixes, mariscos, ou outros produtos animais tais como mel, ovos, leite, manteiga, queijos, ou outros produtos lácteos.

Mas nós comemos: batatas, arroz, macarrão (sem ovos), feijão, vegetais, legumes, tomates, frutas, nozes, cogumelos; pães ou pastéis sem gordura animais ou ovos; cereais/ sucrilhos/ etc.

Sopas e molhos devem ser preparados com caldo de vegetais, nunca com caldo de carne ou galinha. Somente óleo puro vegetal ou margarina pura vegetal devem ser usados no cozimento, nunca manteiga ou qualquer outra gordura animal.

Por favor providencie uma refeição que supra nossos requisitos.

MUITO OBRIGADO

VĂ ROG SĂ CITIȚI

Eu sînt "vegăn" / Noi sîntem "vegăni"
(Pur vegetarian)

Un adevărat vegăn nu mănîncă produse animaliere.

Deci noi nu mîncăm: carne (carne măcinată, cîrnați etc.), păsări (pui, găini etc.), peşte, mîncaruri din peşte, scoici, miere de albine, oua, lapte, unt, caşcaval, sau alte produse lactate.

Dar noi mîncăm: cartofi, orez, paste făinoase (dar fără ouă), fasole, legume, roşii, fructe, nuci, ciuperci, pîine; prăjituri (fără ouă sau grăsime animalieră), cereale şi produse cerealiere.

Supele şi felul 2, noi le preparăm cu ajutorul legumelor fără să folosim carne. În prepararea mîncarurilor noi folosim numai ulei de plante sau margarină produse din legume şi nu folosim unt sau grăsime animalieră.

Vă rog să folosiți rețeta noastră.

VA MULȚUMIM

ПОЖАЛУЙСТА, ПРОЧТИТЕ ЭТО

Я веган / Я веганка / МЫ веганы.

Из принципа веганы не едят никакой пищи животного происхождения на благо людей, животных и окружающей среды.

Итак, мы не едим: мясо (включая блюда из мясного фарша, колбасы, сосиски и т. п.), птицу (включая курицу), рыбу, ракообразных или другие продукты животного происхождения, такие как мед, яйца, молоко, масло, сыр или другие молочные продукты.

Но мы едим: картофелъ, рис, макаронные изделия (на неяичной основе), фасолъ, бобы, овощи, помидоры, фрукты, орехи, грибы, хлеб или выпечные изделия, в состав которых не входит животный жир, каши, крупяные продукты и т. п.

Супы и соусы могут бытъ приготовлены толъко на овощной основе, а не из мясных или куриных экстрактов. При приготовлении пищи может быть использовано только растительное масло или растителъный маргарин, но не сливочное масло или любой другой животный жир.

Пожалуйста, предоставьте еду, которая удовлетворила бы наши потребности.

СПАСИБО

МОЛИМО ВАС ПРОЧТАЈТЕ ОВО ОБАВЕШТЕЊЕ

Ја сам веган / ми смо вегани
(Строги вегетаријанци)

Из принципа, вегани не једу намирнице животињског порекла, за бољу будућност људи, животиња и природе.

Ми не једемо: месо (укључу јући млевено месо, кобасице, паштете, итд), перад (укључу јући пилетину), рибу, шкољке, или друге животињске производе као што су мед, јаја, млеко, маслац, сир, или други млечни произвооди.

Али ми једемо: кромпир, пшринач, тестенину (без јаја), пасуљ, поврће, парадајз, воће, лешике, орахе, печурке; хлеб и пецива или колаче прављене без животињске масти, жштарице производе, итд.

Супе сосеви могу бити спремњени са поврћем али без месних или пилећих пилећих зачина. Само чисто биљно уљв или биљни маргарин може да се употреби у кувању, без маслаца и осталих животињских маслоћа.

Молиьо вас спремите јело по овом упутству.

ХВАЛА

TINA KUMBIRA KUTI MUWERENGE IZVI

Ndiri muvegan / Tiri mavegans

Esu mavegans kudziirira mhukazesango hatidye:

nyama, huku, turkey, huve, mbudzi, nguruwe, tsuru, mhembe, makurwe, matemba, iswa, mbewa, hwiza, zvese dzimbuu dzesango zvese zvinombikwa ne mafutaemhuka; huchi, mazai, mukaka, butter, cheese, cream, yogurt.

Saka tinodya:

matapiri, mupungu, bota, beans, muriwo, madomasi, muchiero ye musango, dzungu, hovea, chingwa, sadza, mafuta endzungu kana masunflower ne 'mabutttercup', muto kwere nyama kana nyama ye huku.

Tino kumbiro kubika zvinyorwa zviri papepa.

TINOTENDA ZVIKURU

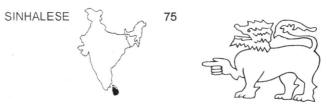

කඳුරුණාකර ගැන කියවන්න.
ළමා කලා ඉදිරිපත්කළේ ඩි. /අයි. අලංක්‍රිප්‍රප්තන් කැරු.

ඈත කාලයේ, සතුන්ගේ හා පරිසරයේ නිසි සමබරතාව පවතා, අපි
පුර්ණ්ශකයක් වෘයෙන්, සත්වසිප් යොත් ලංගයක් ඳිසින්
ඳිලෙනල කලා සිසිත් ආහාරයට භොගානිමු.

එහෙත, අපි පහත සඳහාත් ආහාර වැඩි අනුභව නොකරමු.
යව, එළි, උනද ඇහුළු සියළු ධාන වඩි; තර හා කුකුළු බිජ;
තාර, කරවල හා උප්පිතබඩු; බුන්සේ, දැල්ලෝ, කකුළුවෝ හා
තෙල්ලෝ. සුවද රද පැනි, මිස්තර, සිරි, බවර (සෙවදු), ඔේර
තොයද් හා මුදුවර තිරි හා පෙව්ත අදංගු ආහාරද
ආහාරද (උ.ඳ. තේක, තේරි, වලන්ත) අපි අනුභව නොකරමු.

අපි සුලසක්ශත් පහත සඳහාත් ආහාර වැඩිත් කනති.
තේ ඇහුළු ධාන වඩි; බතල ඇහුළු අල වඩි; සූ, කඳල,
පර්ප්ප අපි අල වඩි; එළවළු හා බහ වඩි; සිර අපි කොළ වඩි;
අලත්තුරු; කල, කුර, කොස අපි ඉඳි අල වඩි; සිසිතර තොඳ
තුඹුර; කාමා රේද තොඳත බඩු ඳත් සත හා තිවිස්; රොද,
අප්ත, ඉඳිආප්ත හා ඳිඹු.

සුත්, ඳොඳි හා සොස් වඩි ඳිඹුයෙත කිරෙදේ, අපි සත්ව මාශ
අංගු සූත් කල තාභිව් තොකරමු. ආකර බද්දන හා
තෝවරණ කිරත සත්ව රේද තො එළෙතසල මයුවත
තෙල්රතෝත්, තෝ එළඟූත් තෙල්, සත්විත කල, හැකිය.

කඳුරුණාකර ගී අනුව අත සුඳුසු නිවස් කළ පෙනුත
ඳිලෝතල කර දෙත්ත.

PROSÍM PREČÍTAJTE SI

Som vegán. / Som vegánka. / Sme vegáni.

V princípe, vegáni nekonzumujú nič, čo je živočíšneho pôvodu, úžitku ľudí, zvierat a životného prostredia.

Nekonzumujeme teda: mäso (ani vo forme fašírok, párkov a podobne), hydinu (vrátane kurčiat), ryby, morské živočíchy a výrobky živočíšneho pôvodu aka sú med, vajcia, mlieko, maslo, syr a iné mliečne výrobky.

Ale konzumujeme: zemiaky, cestoviny (bezvaječné), ryžu, strukoviny, zeleninu, ovocie, orechy, huby, chlieb alebo pečivo vyrobené bez živočíšneho tuku, obilie (ako ovsené vločky a im podobné výrobky), atd.

Polievky a omáčky môžu byť vyrobené z potravín rastlinného pôvodu, ale bez zvyškov mäsa (vrátane hydiny) ako i vývaru. Len čistý rastlinný olej alebo čistý rastlinný margarín môže byť použitý pri varení, žiadne maslo alebo iný živočíšny tuk.

Prosím ponúkite nám jedlo, ktoré spíňa naše požiadavky.

ĎAKUJEME

PROSIMO, PREBERITE SI TO BESEDILO

Jaz sem vegan(ka) / Mi smo vegani

Zaradi lastnega prepričanja vegani ne jemo ničesar, kar je živalskega izvora – zavoljo dobrobiti ljudi, živali in okolja.

Iz tega razloga ne jemo: mesa (vključno z mletim mesom, klobas, itd.), perutnine (vključno s piščanci), rib, morskih sadežev, ali drugih živalskih izdelkov kot so med, jajca, mleko, maslo, sir ali drugih mlečnih proizvodov.

Vendar jemo: krompir, riž, testenine (brez jajc), stročnice, zelenjavo, paradižnik, sadje, oreščke, gobe; kruh in pecivo, izdelano brez živalskih maščob; žitarice in izdelke iz žitaric ipd.

Juhe in omake so lahko pripravljene na zelenjavni osnovi, vendar brez uporabe mesnih ali piščanjih izvlečkov (kock). Za kuho se sme uporabljati le čisto rastlinsko olje ali čista rastlinska margarina, torej brez uporabe masla ali kakršne koli druge živalske maščobe.

Ali nam lahko prosim ponudite obrok, ki zadovoljuje vse naše zahteve?

NAJLEPŠA VAM HVALA!

Waxaan ahay <u>vegan</u>.

Qofka veganka ah, waa qof ka sii xag jira gofka vegetarianka ah, aad iyo aadna uga dheerada hilibka xoolaha oo dhan iyo wixii kale ee xoolaha ka soo baxa ba.

Veganka qofka ah wuxuuna cunin: hilibka xoolaha oo dhan, kalluunka iyo wixii la dhigma, beedka caanaha, jeeska, iyo wixii kale ee xoolaha ka soo baxa.

Wuxuuna cunna: khudrada oo dhan, baradhada, tamaandhada, miraha, bariiska, iyo wixii la dhigma.

Maraga iyo suugada laga sameeyey khudrada ama miraha, kuna jirin, nafaqo xoolaad.

Wixii dubid iyo shiilimaad ah na subag ama saleed laga sameeyey khudrasd ama miro, kuna jirin, nafaqo xoolad.

LE RUEGO QUE LEA ESTA INFORMACIÓN

**Soy vegano / Soy vegana /
Somos veganos / Somos veganas**

Quienes seguimos una dieta vegana no consumimos ningún producto de origen animal y mantenemos una postura ecológicamente responsable de respeto a los seres humanos, los animales y el media ambiente.

Por tanto los veganos/veganas NO comemos: carne (incluida la carne picada y las salchichas), aves de corral (incluidos los pollos), pescado, mariscos u otros productos como la miel, los huevos, la leche, la mantequilla, el queso o cualquier otro producto lácteo.

Los veganos/veganas SÍ comemos: patatas (papas), arroz, pastas alimenticias (sin huevo), legumbres (judías, garbanzos, lentejas, guisantes, etc.), verduras, tomates, fruta, frutos secos, semillas, champiñones, pan o pastelería (preparada sin huevo ni grasa animal), cereales y productos a base de cereales o de soja como el tofu, etc.

Las sopas y salsas se pueden hacer con caldo vegetal, pero no con carne ni extracto de pollo. Para cocinar debe utilizarse siempre aceite puro vegetal o margarina pura vegetal y no la mantequilla ni ninguna otra grasa animal.

**GRACIAS PAR PREPARAR LA COMIDA SEGÚN
NUESTRAS NECESIDADES**

SOMA HAYA TAFADHALI

Mimi ni mvegana / Sisi ni wavegana

Wavegana kwa desturi hawakuli vyakula vyovyote zipatikanalo kwa kuuwauwa, kuchinjwa kwa mnyama, au kutolewa mwilini mwa mnyama kwa njia lolote lile. Sababu ya haya ni kujali masilahi ya binadamu, wanyama na kulinda mazingara yetu.

Kwa hivyo hatuli: nyama yoyote (hata ikiwa nyama-saga, nofo, n.k.); kuku au ndege namna yoyote; samaki; kaa, kamba, chaza, n.k.; au vyakula zilizopatikana kwa kupitia mwilini mwa viumbe K.m. asali, mayai, maziwa, siagi, samli, jbini, n.k.

Vyakula vyetu ni kama haya: viazi, wali, 'pasta' ('K.m. spaghetti, vermicelli, macaroni, n.k.' lisilochanganywa na yai), maharagwe; mboga, nyanya, matunda, njugu, uyoga, sima; kitumbua ama maandazi isiyopikwa na mafuta ya mnyama; nafaka ay vyakula vya chembechembe, n.k.

Supu na mchuzi lililotayarishwa kwa mboga isiyo na nyama, wala sehemu yoyote ya kuku. Ila tu mafuta au siagi halisi ya mboga ndio inawezatumika kuwapikia wavegana vyakula vyao. Vilevile hawatumii siagi wala si mafuta yoyote iliyotayarishwa kutokana na mafuta ya mnyama.

Tafadhali tupe chakula ile itakayoambata na mahitaji yetu.

AHSANTE SANA

VAR VÄNLIG OCH LÄS DETTA.

Jag är vegan / Vi är veganer

Av princip äter inte veganer någonting från djurriket - av omtanke om människor, djur och miljö.

Därför äter vi inte: kött (inklusive köttfärs, korv etc.), kyckling, fisk, skaldjur, kaviar eller andra animaliska produkter sam honung, ägg, mjölk, fil, smör, ost eller andra mjölkprodukter.

Men vi äter: potatis, rig, pasta (utan ägg), bönor, grönsaker, tomater, frukt, nötter, svamp; bröd eller bakverk utan animaliskt fett; säd och sädesprodukter etc.

Soppor och såser kan tillredas av vegetabilisk buljong men inte av kött- eller hönsbuljong. Till matlagning kan vegetabilisk olja eller rent vegetabiliskt margarin (mjölkfritt) användas, inte smör, ister eller annat animaliskt fett.

Var vänlig och laga till en måltid efter våra önskemål.

TACK SÅ MYCKET

MANGYARI LAMANG NA BASAHIN PO ITO

Ako ay vegan / kami ay mga vegan

Sa principyo, ang mga vegan ay hindi kumakain ng anuman na nanggaling sa hayop para sa kapakanan ng mga tao, hayop at ng kapaligiran.

Kaya kami ay hindi kumakain ng: karne (kabilang ang giniling na karne, longganisa at iba pa), manukan (kabilang ang pato, gansa, pabo at iba pa), isda, tulya at suso, o anumang produkto ng hayop katulad ng pulut-pukyutan, itlog, gatas, mantikilya, keso, o anuman na gawa sa gatas.

Pero kami ay kumakain ng: patatas, kanin, pasta (katulad ng pansit, macaroni, spagetti at iba pa na walang halong itlog), bins o lentehas (katulad ng munggo, patani, at iba pa), gulay, kamatis, prutas, kabute, tinapay o kakanin na walang halong mantika ng baboy, seryal at ang mga produkto nito

Ang mga sabaw at sawsawan ay maaring gawa sa katas ng gulay pero hindi sa sabaw ng manok o karne. Purong mantikang gulay o purong margarinang gulay lamang ang maaring gamitin sa pagluluto, hindi ang mantikilya o mantikang-hayop.

Mangyari lamang na bigyan ninyo ako/kami ng pagkain na alinsunod sa aming mga kinakailangan.

SALAMAT PO

காய்கனியர் கடவுச்சீட்டு.

தயவுசெய்து இதை படியுங்கள்

நான் ஒரு காய்கனியர் / நாங்கள் காய்கனியர்கள்.

காய்கனியர்கள் கொள்கைப் படி விலங்குகளை சார்ந்த எதையும் உட்கொள்ள மாட்டார்கள். இது மக்கள், விலங்கினம் மற்றும் சுற்றுப்புறச்சூழலின் நலனைக் கருதி.

அதனால் நாங்கள் உட்கொள்ளாதது :- இறைச்சி (துண்டாக்கப்பட்ட இறைச்சி, சாஸெக உட்பட) கோழிப்பண்ணை உற்பத்தி (கோழிஇறைச்சி உட்பட), மீன், ஓடுடைய மீன் (ஆளி, கடற்காய், நண்டு, மட்டி, முத்துச்சிப்பி) மற்றும் பிற விலங்கினஉற்பத்தி தேன், முட்டை, பால், வெண்ணெய், பாற்கட்டி, தயிர், நெய் மற்றும் பால்பண்ணை விளைபொருள்.

ஆனால் நாங்கள் உட்கொள்வது :- உருளைக்கிழங்கு, அரிசி, பாஸ்தா (முட்டை இல்லாதது), பீன்ஸ், காய்கறிவகைகள், தக்காளி, கனிகள், கொட்டைவகைகள், காளான், ரொட்டி, கேக் (விலங்குகளின் கொழுப்புச்சத்து இல்லாமல்) தானியம் மற்றும் தானியவிளைபொருள்.

காய் ரசம் (சூப்பு) மற்றும் சாஸ்வகைகள் காய்கறிகலவைகளால் செய்யப்பட்டு ஆனால் இறைச்சி மற்றும் கோழிஇறைச்சிவடிமம் சேர்க்காதது. சுத்தமான தாவர எண்ணெய் அல்லது சுத்தமான தாவர மார்கரினால் சமையல் செய்யப்படலாம் ஆனால் வெண்ணெய், நெய் அல்லது விலங்குகளின் கொழுப்பு கட்டாயமாக பயன்படுத்தக்கூடாது.

தயவுசெய்து எங்கள் தேவைக்கேற்ற உணவை உங்களால் எங்களுக்கு அளிக்க முடியுமா ?

மிக்க நன்றி.

విజ్ఞాపన పత్రము

దయచేసి ఈ పత్రమును చదవండి.

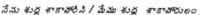
నేను శుద్ధ శాకాహారిని / మేము శుద్ధ శాకాహారులం

ప్రజల, జంతువుల మరియు పర్యావరణం యొక్క ప్రయోజనం కోసం శుద్ధ శాకాహారులమైన నేను / మేము జంతు సంబంధిత పదార్థములను తినను / తినము.

నేను / మేము తినని పదార్థములు : అన్ని రకముల మాంసము మరియు జంతు సంబంధిత పదార్థములైన తేనె, గుడ్లు, పాలు, పెరుగు, మజ్జిగ, వెన్న, నెయ్యి, జున్ను మొదలైనవి.

నేను / మేము తినే పదార్థములు : అన్నము, రొట్టెలు, కూరగాయలు, ఆకుకూరలు, పండ్లు, పుట్ట గొడుగులు, జీడి పప్పు, బాదం పప్పు, ఖర్జూర, ఎండు ద్రాక్ష, తృణ ధాన్యములతో చేసిన అల్పాహార ములు (ఇడ్లీ, దోశ, పూరీ, వడ, ఉప్మా మొదలైనవి).

పులుసులు, పప్పు చారు మరియు రసం తయారు చేయునప్పుడు ఉపయోగించు నీరు మంచి నీరైన లేక కూరగాయలు ఉడికించిన నీరైన అయి ఉండవలెను.

వంటకు మొక్కల యొక్క గింజల నుండి తీసిన శుద్ధమైన నూనె(పేరు శనగ, నువ్వులు, పొద్దు తిరుగుడు, తవుడు, మొక్క జొన్న మొదలైనవి) మాత్రమే ఉపయోగించవలెను.

దయచేసి పైన పేర్కొనిన పదార్థములతో చేసిన వంటను / భోజనమును / అల్పాహారమును వడ్డించగలరా?

ధన్యవాదములు

กรุณาอ่านข้อความต่อไปนี้

ดิฉัน/ผม เป็นชาวมังสวิรัติที่เคร่งครัด / เราเป็นชาวมังสวิรัติที่เคร่งครัด

โดยหลักการแล้ว
ชาวมังสวิรัติที่เคร่งครัดจะไม่รับประทานอาหารชนิดใดทั้งสิ้นที่ทำมาจากสัต
ว์ ทั้งนี้ เพื่อผลดีต่อมนุษย์ สัตว์ และสิ่งแวดล้อม

ดังนั้นเราจึงไม่รับประทานอาหารดังต่อไปนี้
เนื้อสัตว์ (เนื้อบด เนื้อสัตว์ทุกชนิด เช่น เนื้อแพะ เนื้อวัว เนื้อหมู ไส้กรอก
ฯลฯ) สัตว์ปีก เช่นไก่ เป็ด นก รวมทั้งปลา ปู กุ้ง หอย และผลิตผลจากสัตว์
เช่น น้ำผึ้ง ไข่ น้ำนม เนย เนยแข็ง หรือผลผลิตอื่นๆจากนมวัว

เรารับประมานอาหารต่อไปนี้
มันฝรั่ง ข้าว เส้นหมี่ (ไม่ผสมไข่) ก๋วยเตี๋ยว ถั่วต่างๆ ผัก มะเขือเทศ ผลไม้
เมล็ดถั่ว เห็ด ขนมปัง หรือแป้งซึ่งไม่มีส่วนผสมของไขมันสัตว์ ซีรีล
และผลผลิตจากพืชพันธุ์ธัญญาหารที่ทำจากเมล็ดพืช เป็นต้น

น้ำซุปและซอสสามารถทำได้จากน้ำผัก แต่ต้องไม่ใช่ที่เคี่ยวมาจากเนื้อสัตว์
หรือเนื้อไก่ ในการประกอบอาหารให้ใช้น้ำมันพืชแท้ๆ
หรือเนยเทียมที่ทำจากพืช ไม่ใช่เนย หรือไขมันสัตว์อื่นๆ

ถ้าเป็นไปได้ ขอความกรุณาจัดอาหารที่ถูกต้องตามความต้องการให้เราด้วย

ขอบคุณมากค่ะ / ครับ

 ཕྱོགས་རྗེས་ག་ཟིགས་འདི་སྐྱོག་རོགས་གནང་
བདག་ནི་སྟོ་ཟབས་པ་ཞིག་ཡིན། ཆུག་ཆག་ནི་སྟོ་ཟབས་པ་རྣམས་ཡིན།
རུ་འཛིན་ནམ་དག་བཅའ་ནི། སྟོ་ཟབས་པ་རྣམས་ཀྱིས་མི་དང་སེམས་ཅན་འཁོར་ཡུག་བཅས་ཀྱི་ཁེ་
ཕན་གྱི་ཆེད་དུ་སེམས་ཅན་གྱི་འབྱུང་ཁུངས་ལོངས་སུ་སྤྱོད་མི་རུང་།
དེས་ན་ང་ཚོས་ཕ་དང་ཕའི་ཆར་གཏོགས་གཙོ་བས་ཕ་དང་ཕ་རྒྱལ་སོགས་པ་དང་། བུ་ཕ་དང་
བུ་ཕའི་ཆར་གཏོགས། ཁྱིམ་བུ། ས། ཉི་ཕྱིས་ལ་སོགས་པ་དང་། གཞན་ཡང་སེམས་ཅན་
གཞན་ལས་བྱུང་བ། དཔེར་ན། སྤྲང་རྩི། སྦྲང་། འོ་མ། སྨར། ཕུར་བ་ལ་སོགས་པ་དང་།
གཞན་པའི་མའི་ཐོན་རྫས་སོགས་ལོངས་སུ་སྤྱོད་མི་རུང་།

ང་ཚོས་ལོངས་སུ་སྤྱོད་རུང་བ་ནི། ཞིག་གོག་འབྲས། སྟོང་མེ་ཐུག་པ། སྲན་མ། སྟོ་
ཚོད་རྣམས། ཏོ་མ་ཏོ། ཤིང་ཏོག་རིགས། སྤར་ཁ། གཙོག་བག་ལེབ། ཚིལ་མེ་དགྲ་སྒྲིག
འབྲུ་རིགས། འབྲུ་རིགས་ཀྱི་ཕོན་ཟས་ལ་སོགས་པའོ།

ཁུ་བ་དང་སྐྱོ་རྣམས་གཅིག་བྱས་ན་ཚོད་བཅུད་ཀྱིས་བཟོ་ཚོག་ཕོད་དང་བུ་ག སཔྲུའི་མནས
དུ་བཟོ་མི་རུང་། དེལ་སྐྱུ་རྒྱུ་པ་འབའ་འབྱམར་རྣམས་ད་ལལ་ཞལ་ལག་གནད་དུ་སྤྱོད་ཚོག མར
དང་སེམས་ཅན་གཞན་གྱི་ཚིལ་སྐྱུ་སོགས་བེད་སྤྱོད་གཏོང་མི་རུང་།

ཕྱོགས་རྗེས་ག་ཟིགས་ཁྱིད་ཀྱིས་ང་ཚོའི་དགོས་མཁོ་ལ་གང་འོས
འཚམས་ཀྱི་ཞལ་ལག་ཞིག་མཁོ་སྤྱོད་ཐུབ་བས།

ཉིན་དུ་ཕྱོགས་རྗེ་ཚེ་ཞུ་རྒྱུ་ཡིན།།

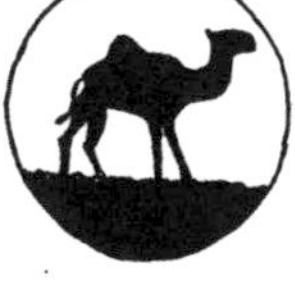

LÜTFEN BUNU OKUR MUSUNUZ?

Ben bir veganım / Biz veganız
(Toprakürünü yiyenleriz)

İlke olarak veganlar insanlar, hayvanlar ve çevre yararı için hayvansal madde veya hayvansal maddeden yapılan hiçbirşey yemezler.

Böylece biz şunları yemeyiz: et (kıyma, sucuk dahil), tavuk (av kuşu dahil), balık (balık yağı dahil) ve hayvansal deniz ürünleri (midye, ıstakoz, kalamar gibi) veya öteki hayvansal maddeler (bal, yumurta, süt, tereyağı, kaymak, hellim, yoğurt, ayran, sütlü tatlılar gibi bütün süt mamülleri).

Ama şunları yeriz: patates, pirinç (sade yağsız, et suyusuz), makarna (et suyusuz, yumurtasız), fasulye, ve mercimek gibi baklagiller; sebze (tomates, mantar, kollandro, meyve) fındık, leblebi gibi kuruyemişler, ekmek, erişte gibi hamur ürünleri (etsiz, peynirsiz, yumurtasız, tereyağsız, sütsüz), tahıl ve tahılsal ürünler (buğday, arpa vs) gibi bütün toprak ürünleri.

Çorba ve soslar sebzelerin kaynatıldığı suda yapılabılır ama etsuyu, tavuksuyu kesinlikle kullanılamaz. Yemekler sadece saf bitkisel yağ (zeytin, ay çiçeği gibi) kullanılarak pişirilmeli ve asla tereyağı, margarin, kuyruk yağı, balık yağı kullanilmamalıdır. Sebzeler katiyen etle pişirilmemeli, et yemeğinin içine sokulan kaşık iyice ternizlenmeden kullanilmamalıdır.

Lütfen bizim isteklerimize uygun bir yemek hazırlar mısınız?

ÇOK TEŞEKKÜRLER

БУДЬ ЛАСКА ПРОЧИТАЙТЕ ЦЕ

Я – строгий вегетаріанець / Ми – строгі вегетаріанці

Строгі вегетаріанці принципово не їдять нічого з продуктів тваринного походження — на користь людям, тваринам і навколишньому середовищу.

Отож ми не їмо: м'яса (включаючи рублене м'ясо, ковбасу, сосиски та інше), птицю (включаючи курятину), рибу, молюсків або інші продукти тваринного походження, такі як мед, яйця, молоко, масло, сир та інші молочні продукти.

Але ми їмо: картоплю, рис, макарони (без вмісту яєць), боби, овочі, томати, фрукти, горіхи, гриби, хліб та печиво без вмісту тваринних жирів; крупи та круп'яні продукти, тощо.

Супи та соуси можуть бути зроблені на овочевій основі але не з екстрактами м'яса або курятини. Тільки чиста рослинна олія може бути використана для приготування їжі, але не вершкове масло або інший тваринний жир.

Будь ласка, чи зможете ви забезпечити нам їжу, яка відповідає нашим вимогам?

ЩИРО ВАМ ВДЯЧНІ

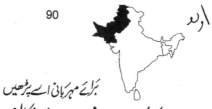

برائے مہربانی اسے پڑھیں

میں خالص سبزی خور ہوں / ہم خالص سبزی خور ہیں

اصولی طور پر ہم خالص سبزی خور لوگ کسی بھی قسم کے جانوروں کا گوشت اور جانوروں سے متعلق اشیاء نہیں کھاتے ہیں ۔ یہ انسانوں، جانوروں اور ہمارے ماحول کے تحفظ کی ایک کوشش ہے ۔ اس لئے ہم یہ اشیاء نہیں کھاتے ہیں ۔

گوشت (ہر قسم کے جانوروں کا گوشت، مرغ اور تمام پرندوں کا گوشت، مچھلی، جھینگے وغیرہ تمام جانوروں سے متعلق اشیاء جیسے شہد، انڈے، دودھ، دہی، مکھن، خالص گھی اور دودھ سے تیار کی ہوئی اشیاء ۔ وہ مٹھائیاں جو کھویا یا مالٹا دودھ سے تیار کی جاتی ہیں ۔ ہم دودھ سے بنی چائے، کافی لسی یا ملک شیک استعمال نہیں کرتے ہیں۔ لیکن ہم یہ چیزیں کھاتے ہیں ۔

ہر قسم کی سبزیاں، ترکاریاں، آلو گبھیوں، چاول، دالیں، ٹماٹر، پھل، روٹی اور اناج سے تیار کی ہوئی وہ اشیاء جن میں جانوروں کی چربی یا دودھ وغیرہ کا استعمال نہ کیا گیا ہو ۔ بغیر دودھ کی چائے، کافی، پھلوں کا رس، یا لیموں کا شربت وغیرہ ہم استعمال کر سکتے ہیں۔

شوربے اور سوپ وغیرہ بھی نباتاتی اجزاء سے تیار شدہ کھاتے جا سکتے ہیں۔ لیکن اگر اس میں گوشت یا مرغ وغیرہ کے اجزاء کا استعمال کیے گئے بنائیں تو وہ ہم نہیں کھا سکتے ۔ کھانے میں نباتاتی تیل استعمال کیا جا سکتا ہے ۔ کھانا تیار کرنے کے لئے ممکن اور کسی بھی جانوروں کی چربی کا استعمال نہ کیا جائے

۔۔: ہماری گذارش ہے کہ :۔

برائے مہربانی : ہماری ان ضروریات کے مطابق ہمیں کھانا فراہم کریں ۔

۔: شکریہ :۔

Xin Qúy Vị Hãy Dọc Những Lời Sau Đây.

Tôi là một ngỹời ân chay. / Chúng tôi ăn chay trỹờng.

Trên nguyên tắc, ăn chay trỹờng trong bữa – ăn không có thịt mục đích để bảo vệ đời sống của con ngỹời và thiên nhiên.

Chúng tôi không ăn thịt (gồm có thịt bằm, thịt dời, lạp xỹởng), gà vịt, tôm cá, nghêu sò; hoặc là những sản phẩm do thú vật sản xuất nhỹ trứng, sữa, mật ong …

Chúng tôi ăn khoai tây, gạo, bún, đậu, rau, cà chua, trái cây, nấm, bánh mì, và bánh ngọt không có chất béo cýa thú vật, không có trứng, không có sữa.

Canh và nýớc dùng có thể nấu bằng rau chứ đừng làm bằng nýớc cốt thịt bò, gà hay cá – cũng đừng dùng Viandox hay dầu hào. Đồ xào hay chiên đừng dùng bỡ hay chất mỡ nào lấy từ thú vật mà chỉ dùng dầu lấy từ cây quả.

Xin quý vị đề nghị một bữa cõm hợp với bài viết ở trên đây.

Cám õn nhiều lắm

DARLLENWCH HWN OS GWELWCH YN DDA

Rydw i'n figan / Rydym ni'n figaniaid (llysieuwyr caeth)

Fel mater o egwyddor, ni fydd figaniaid yn bwyta unrhyw beth sy'n dod o anifeiliaid - er lles pobl, anifeiliaid a'r amgylchedd.

Felly ni fyddwn ni'n bwyta: cig (gan gynnwys briwgig, selsig ayb.), ieir (gan gynnwys cyw iâr), pysgod, pysgod cregyn, na chynnyrch arall o anifeiliaid megis mêl, wyau, llaeth, menyn, caws na chynnyrch llaeth arall.

Ond byddwn ni'n bwyta: tatws, reis, pasta (heb wyau), ffa, llysiau, tomatos, ffrwythau, cnau, madarch; bara a chrwst wedi'i wneud heb fraster anifeiliaid; grawnfwyd a chynnyrch grawn, ayb.

Mae modd gwneud cawl a saws gyda gwlych llysiau ond nid gyda rhin cig na chyw iâr. Dim ond olew llysiau pur neu margarîn llysiau pur ellir ei ddefnyddio wrth goginio, nid menyn na saim o anifeiliaid.

Os gwelwch chi'n dda, fedrwch chi ddarparu pryd o fwyd sy'n ateb ein gofynion?

DIOLCH YN FAWR IAWN

JOWO KA IMORAN ISALE YI

Ajeso-nikan ni mi, nko jeran / Ajeso-nikan ni wa, a ko jeran

Nitori ajeso-nikan ni wa, a ti pinnu pe a ko ni je eran rara – fun anfani awon enia, eranko, ati ayika aye.

Nitori idi eyi a ko ki nje: eran (eran bokoto, saki, ati bebe lo) eran adiye (pelu tolotolo), eja, eja onike, tabi awon eya eranko bi oyin, eyin, miliki, bota, wara oyinbo, tabi awon ohun ara maalu.

Sugbon a ma nje: anomo, iresi, pasita, ewa, efo, tomato, orombo tabi osan, eyin, mosurumu, buredi tabi akara oyinbo ti ko ni ora eran ninu, sirili ati awon onje ti a fi agbado tabi oka baba se, ati bebe lo.

A ko le je obe ti o ni eran nomo tabi adiye ninu re ayafi obe efo tabi ila/ewedu (ati bebe lo) nikan. A ko le lo ororo ti o wa lati inu bota tabi eran nomo/adiye ayafi epo pupa tabi ororo lati inu egunsi nikan.

Jowo, se o le se tabi ta onje ti o tele awon alaye ti a se soke iwe yi mu fun wa bi?

A DUPE LOWO RE PUPO PUPO

BONVOLU LEGI ĈI TION

Mi estas vegan(in)o / Ni estas vegan(in)oj

(vegetalanoj)

Pro principo, veganoj manĝas nenion el animala origino – por la bono de homoj, bestoj kaj la medio.

Do, ni ne manĝas: viandon (inklusive de viandmuelitaĵo, kolbaso, ktp), kortobirdaĵon (inklusive de kokinaĵo), fiŝon, konkulojn, aŭ aliajn animalproduktaĵojn kiel mielon, ovojn, lakton, buteron, froamaĝon aŭ iu ajn laktaĵon.

Sed ni ja manĝas: terpomojn, rizon, pastaĵon (sen ovo), fazeolojn, legomojn, tomatojn, fruktojn, nuksojn, fungojn; panon aŭ kukojn faritaj sen animala graso; grenon kaj grenproduktaĵojn, ktp.

Supoj kaj saŭcoj ne infuziĝu el viando, kortobirdaĵo, aŭ io tia, seed jes el legomoj. Nur pure vegetala oleo aŭ pure vegetala margarino uziĝu por juirado, kaj ne el butero aŭ el alia animalaj grasoj.

Mi (ni) petas, ĉu vi provizi (nin) per manĝoj, kiuj plenumu miajn (niajn) bezonojn?

DANKON

The Vegan Society is always pleased to hear of any corrections or improvements to the translations in this book, and to receive any offers of translation into languages not already included.

If you can help in any of these ways, please contact

The Vegan Society

Donald Watson House

21 Hylton Street

Hockley

Birmingham

B18 6HJ

United Kingdom

Tel: 0121 523 1730

E-mail: info@vegansociety.com

IF ALL ELSE FAILS!

IF ALL ELSE FAILS!

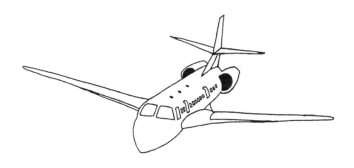

VGML

Vegan airline meal code   **Код бортового питания для веганов**

纯素食者航空餐饮代码

ভিগান এয়ারলাইনের খাদ্যনীতি   **Spezialmenü-Buchungscode**

Código para refeição vegan das companhias aéreas

Code IATA repas végétalien   वीगन एयरलाइन भोजन सुचकांक

رمز وجبات طعام خطوط الطيران للغذاء النباتي
(الخال من جميع مشتقات الحيوانات بما في ذلك البيض ومشتقات الحليب).

Código comida vegana línea aérea   **Kodo manĝa vegana aerlinia**

ヴィーガン（完全菜食）の航空機内食記号

INDEX

INDEX

INDEX

Food · Drink · Clothing · Household Goods · Personal Care

8th EDITION

Animal Free Shopping
has always been a
way of life for me;
it is the most
compassionate
statement a
shopper can make.
Benjamin Zephaniah